SILENCE OF MEMORY

Serge Gavronsky

Spuyten Duyvil   New York City

ISBN 978-0-9661242-7-9

Library of Congress Cataloging-in-Publication Data

Gavronsky, Serge.
  Silence of memory / Serge Gavronsky.
    pages cm
  ISBN 978-0-9661242-7-9
  I. Title.
  PS3557.A957S55 2014
  811'.54--dc23

                              2014009534

Silence of Memory
Serge Gavronsky

On Gavronsky

Harold Bloom

Within that historical period that we have to refer to as the Age of Terrorism, Serge Gavronsky's *German Friend* is impressive in its timeliness. I re-read it these past days, in light of the direct consequences of the U.S. air strike on Libya [1986]. Gavronsky provides us with a representation of a quality of the mind, which is by no means limited only to those Western extremisms that supported the Terror with the assumption of one or another cause or ideology, but in reality had the only purpose of fostering the Terror, both metaphysically, sexually, and religiously. Although his characters stand on that remote margin, their theosophy of violence has contaminated an entire continuum of the new generation.

Yesterday I walked into an on campus bar, here at Yale, and I took part in a conversation between younger students, who all graduated in literature and had been my students in the past. In reaction to the American air attack, they all condemned it. When I reminded them of some recent examples of terrorism, such as the explosion on an airliner, which had thrown out of the aircraft a grandmother and a mother with her young daughter, they argued with vehemence that such actions were understandable and human, while the American air strike was not. According to them, Palestinians, Libyans, Lebanese, Iranians, and Syrians—not to mention Germans, French, and Irish, would all be "freedom fighters": frustrated, sincere, and misunderstood idealists. On the other hand, the president of the United States and his pilots would be would be professional murderers. The twenty years I spent listening to the judgments of young people in Western universities have not completely hardened me; yet, the trauma of my wonder is not anymore as great as it used to be.

As I re-read the *German Friend*, I hear again that ironic and enigmatic voice of the novelist who is able to absorb nihilism without sinking into it. Gavronsky is the last heir of Conrad, of the most restless and disturbing Conrad, the prophet of the *Secret Agent* and *Under Western Eyes*. Even if in some points it could seem that Gavronsky does not yet fully master the art of writing, he has managed to make an impressive entrance in this way, while adding his own nuances to the ever developing tradition of the political novel.

Bakunin, the patron saint of the terrorists, professed that the passion for destruction was a creative one. Gavronsky, as he alludes to Bakunin's moral idiocy, shows us over and over again that the frustration of terrorists brings with itself the arrest of every creative impulse and of any perception of human diversity. Blake thought that everything somebody could believe in was an image of Truth; however, we constantly see that such statement does not apply to the age we live in as terrorists and those who support them believe only in the impulse of death.

Gavronsky's main theme is, indeed, the impulse of death. With a surprising rhetoric of detachment, he discovered the link between the moral self-justification of the terrorist and the detours to death, which Freud explored more in depth in the essay, *Group Psychology and the Analysis of the Ego*, with the difference, of course, that Freud was not making reference to terrorism as such. The implicit heart of Gavronsky's imaginary meditation lies in the daunting similarity of the dialogues on the two fronts of the war between terror and authority. While we are overwhelmed by the

recitation of the police investigating officers and by the misunderstand-
ings of the parents, we gradually come to understand that the impulse of
death dominates both sides and we do not recognize anymore the bound-
aries between the forms of society and the forms of rebellion.

We can hope that Gavronsky would continue with the novel, but we
also have to hope that he would divert his Balzacian taste from the harass-
ing thought of nihilism.

The great virtue of this novel is also its main defect: his characters
converge because this is the trend that the author discovers in the sexual
metaphysics of terror, which aims at reducing all differences and at bring-
ing the organic to the inorganic.

I pay tribute to Gavronsky and I praise him, urging him at the same
time to return to Balzac's "visio," in the same way Baudelaire caught sight
of it in a world where every porter is a genius.

Is this a novel?

This is one of Pascal's Thoughts:
"Silence eternal frightens me."

THE SILENCE OF MEMORY
(Silence, be not proud)

Aristotle writes: "Every poem is a community of sorts..."
Mallarmé writes: "Hier! Hier! Il est bien loin."
(Was my memory held hostage?)

"Hey, Dude, dontcha know, life's a nightmare."
(Haint dat de trooth?)

First, what seemed to be a rocking of words rocking

Interrupted

Voices against

You might, maybe, you might guess

The captain straightened out his blue coat

Cap on a
bench

Mershaune

 Upsetting rollicking words Herbert
Spencer writes: "The ship's He…" seizes
the wheel
Turns it this way

His hands cold as water

Thought of the ship

Impact of the sea

Clenches his hands
(Question: Where did the "real" go?)
Nearby, a seascape jitters the waves The
captain's blue buttons
Scratch the floor

Perhaps scratches the floor

(He remembers a senior high school dance

Chairs cleared

Cleared them out to let us dance the Cha cha cha imported from

Florida where grand-parents play canasta.)
                              Amos Oz writes: "We
walked in the dark." He mumbles
              As if nothing was

              Had been marked on a nautical map

              A friend salutes

A lieutenant says:

"O! Captain! my captain: We'll pull through."

              Overhears voices

Scratchy combat voices

              The ship pummeled by gigantic waves

The undertow menaces kids

              Parents sing off key

              Wood gathered

On a Labor Day week-end

The captain scratches out

Words on his log

His name, he thinks, is Poplin

If we don't do it

Somebody will read my...
Much later
At the naval academy, a retired captain

Calls attention to his mistakes

Reluctantly, the chaplain bows his head

Holds his leather Bible

(He's done it so many times...
Burials happen on rainy days)

(Black outfit)

A little before the burial

        Max Horkheimer writes: "Ces contradictions appa-
raîssent clairement… "

        The captain's wife stares

        The coffin's nailed

        Says I can't go on

        If a shark bit off his head
        She glances at the ma-
        rines Rifles at the ready
                Jeffrey Masson writes post-Freud:
"….." "Hold on," she screams. "I want to add…"
She CAPTURES the captain's head

                Tick Tick Tick
                Tick (LIKE-
                LIKELIKE)

(What's that ticking sound?
He's wearing a 1940 Bulova.
I have forehearing. Soon you'll hear Marclay watches or was
it all a   premonition of

5

death? death itself publicity.)

We succeeded in OPENING the shark's mouth

His imagined head fell on the deck. She catches a
taxi, screams
"To the taxidermist."

Kaieteur.")
("If you want to eat shark, order it from

Try Murray's.")   ("Otherwise, if you prefer sturgeon,

Once there, she says a new head

Bring it

Remove the nails

The glass coffin stripped of its nails

She cements glue on his sloppy neck

chanter."   Lautréamont writes: "I hear voices," then adds: "let me

She displaces the undertaker

Devastated

Others stare at the captain

The grave is vertical

(Ain't he jus look' in fine?) Rehearsed
 3 hours ago Drums roll
Rifles above the hole

Flowers

A gurgle

Sharks grazed his hand

Poplin says: "There's so little time left..." Everyone
weeps
The flag's folded

        Given to the weeping widow. The trum-
peter goes bassoon. Goes bassoon.
                            Gertrude Stein writes: "Now
                    Not now. Now"
Little do they realize CIA HQ

is
Below
Arling-
ton
Cem-
etery
Sudden-
ly the
earth
opens
up They
drop
kick the
vertical
coffin
Much to
every-
one's
surprise
How!
How!
How!
I told
you:
Poops
(tickticktick: Like Like Like)

The coffin splits open

A fire breaks out Switches places Jumps sideways Salutes
Drowns next to his captain

Then, silence
or that's what people call it. (On the 3rd floor, a
trombone)
In unison, bullets fly

Three naked women

(As in a OO7)

Sing in husky voices

                              "Empty spaces of the mind"

(Where…?)

On the shore, parents sing around a campfire

Sing…
A Holy Mass kids Run around
not far from The vertical hole
Headless head
Up side down.

            Maurice Roche writes: "Il n'y avait personne…"
Daddy, can we throw pebbles on it?

        "Mehr licht" (Goethe writes, with his last breath of

breath. Then asks someone to turn on the night light.)

Slurprized?

Stones kicked over the grave

Wife flips

Can't be happening

Says the admiral, shaken out of bed

The wife says I can't

Please... Let's
finish
A limousine

There's a chauffeur

Dressed as a sailor

Victor Lazlo sings: "La Marseillaise." He
opens three doors
Three naked women

The captain's wife

Off we go to some other place

Cocktails and sandwiches à la française.
"Flowers wilt, dontcha know?"
Everyone important weeps

2 men touch hands

Recite:

Reed."

(She soaks her underwear.)

La Fontaine's gay: "The Oak and the

Sweats, says:

French rouge, please French
powder, please Underarm
Chanel, please

More of everything, please

A shot of cassis

A shot of white wine

Sounds of a bugle

Not on your life

What a shot, Ladies, don't move an inch

good?

Aint she smells

space…"

The trumpeter goes bananas

Don't move

Picabia writes: "… for a larger

Zooms in and out

Shoul-
ders
the
beach
Tour-
ists

glare Red alert
 Bathing suits drop

Another shot, ladies,

They call in the Mentalist

        Nabokov writes: "Poetry as dialectical
materialism."

                itself." Anaïs Nin writes: "All poetry has an image of

        Plato writes: "No, certainly not…" "I
know you can
Do it. Please, "for us."

"Please."

You can imagine

A flash Gordon

                                        nightmare

                        Backdrop with no images a

Tourists on rented bikes

Bound to die, cycle

On the wrong side

(All of a sudden, memory disputes the boundaries of dark-
ened penumbra.) (Between shadows, memory tries to find itself, but, in the
meantime, silence is terrifying…)

Where then-all of a sudden- the earth reopens a CSI in Antigua,
where drugs (Eric Clapton's rehab. In Antigua)
(Jethro Gibbs) Hide below casino tables.
An Italian tourist says in Italian: "I'll be quiet."

A killer shark pops up near a huge tourist ship

400O Italians on a tourist ship

Wheelchairs

Nurses at the ready

Location of the nearest cemetery

Cremation

Lacan writes : "Play it again, Sam… " The
lieutenant drowns next to his Poplin (a mistake?)
A Holy Mass a distance away "Cap-
tain," the lieutenant says "Check
out that burning ship off To the left
there's only… "
(CSI collapses NY and l.A.)

The captain's shoes are locked in

Water

At 7 o'clock, then again at 11, on some TV program,

Guess what the Lieutenant is going to say

In the light above the water

That shark got away

Now, a close up of the headless

 Off to the right

Somebody yells: "Go to bed,hell!
Once more," says the same, trou-
bling the underground The killer

shark gets away Tough luck
      Trotsky writes in Mexico: "Hey, Breton! Watcha you got

cookin?"

The captain's body floats

 Waits for a doctor

A nurse a sonogram

 Nobody knows the trouble he's seen:

      Picabia writes: "If this is a pohem, sum it up"
      (The captain's head bubbles up.)

      English muffins +marmalade She stares at silent
waters Fishermen cast
Nets.
Colors fade. Who can remember... Hoping to
bypass Greek olive oil
(By the by, do you remember last night?) You
can barely hear them---
Oysters condemned to a soaky death A
chef quotes his "adopted" father: "Cut off
the green
A leek is a

Leek."

Not too long ago, the captain, underground, Can't
fight sharks around him

Lacan writes: "Talk in short   figures..."

His wife slides into a black limousine

Flowers wilt

Never think flowers mean death

The wife grows blue roses

                    Jürgen Habermas interrupts:

He quotes, but shakes his head in
German.

John R. Searle writes: "An essay
in the philosophy of poetry."

Ever so quietly, blue simmers a poem

On the surface

Blood-like False
teeth Mean Con-
cepts
ain't dat de trooph? Time
before the burial
A graduate out of Annapolis

Nobody suspects, enumerates:

1. Marxism in Japan

2. Social critique of Italian Marxism at the end of WW II

3. Liberalism in civil societies

4. Merdre on all the above

5. Check out feminism in French films

6. On page 88, write something appropriate

7. On his own, listens to his speech downtoon

8. Social thought as a form of reproduction

9. Read Derrida's Marx's ghost

memory? (expunged...)

Did it ever cross your dream-

     bedbug." Vladimir Mayakovsky writes: "Poetry is a

   "Our captain's
   death..." Got that?
   Thereafter: Wow! Get this.
   Slip it in somewhere...
   CIA--
   Elevators at a standby

   "Captain Poplin, what's my
   grade?" Never did
   Come up with an answer,

   Except for the "social" uncon-
scious. Is there meaning
   In black limousines near a hole?

  (The President, on the lawn of the White
    House,

 Turns to his Press Secretary ." I've done this so many times, still
I can't remember. I can't even recall the name of the last burial.
The Press Secretary says: "You say your memory isn't as good as
it had been a couple of funeral ago. Did you ever consider

symptoms …Try fighting back! Take up your Responsability. Control
yourself and express your condolences…"
"A great American has just passed away."
Others gather around the pit. (The ticking sound…)
"To his country, we raise our plastic glasses."

Flags at half mast

A light rain

Pictures on the sill

Don't move Don't
look Don't wince
Christian MARCLAY says: "Mirages and sounds we're all
familiar with and

Reorganize watches in an unfamiliar…" Nails
are effective
You fuckin' idiot

I told you to keep the shark's

Mouth open.
There's the Sea.
We're standing at attention

Lights over the sunny hole

The widow smiles. It's nearly over

They're about to shovel earth

On the vertical when:

     Giorgio Agamben writes: "Take a step back-
wards, read poetry."

How tall was the captain without a
head? Ask Batman or Robin.
(Check out "Nudi-
ties") The govern-
ment will pin
The Congressional Medal of Honor

 On his left lapel.

Someone sings: "Bee Bop! Goodie
Goodie!" The sea smells rhythmically
A firing squad stands at the ready

                          time."
     Walter Benjamin writes: "The shape of Poetry's

Nobody notices

     Can't

read. A sailor whips out a revolver
Sings the "International."

Remembers his last wish: "Get me

       Frank Sinatra's: "I love you I love you." She holds a gradu-
       ation picture, he's 6'4

She stares at the captain's headless,

Asks a limo to drive her to the nearest taxidermist,

Holds the photograph. "Here," she says.

"Make him a new head, symbolic, but do it." She
whispers: "jouissance."
With cement glue glues it on

His headless neck. In the meantime,

Somebody spots spermy spots

       Eisenstein says: " Poetry is a
pumpkin. " Then adds:

       "Potemkin."

Nobody could write as well as Shelley:

                                                        Mankind."
"Poetry is the acknowledged legislator of

        "Wow," says the lieutenant.

        In a Moroccan film, a skinny guy

                                                        this…"
Sings: "You must remember

        And adds: "A coffin is just
        a coffin." "That's all, folks.
        Certain thoughts are better…Then others. Shut your eyes."

                                "Ah!
                Merz…" Blimpie says : " Po-
                etry is scrumptious."
        (Hell's a Poplin.)

Poplin is escorted to the 5th floor of the Pentagon's Soviet Research

Center:

                Wears a see-
                through mask

Wears surgeon's gloves

Wears a see-through plastic suit

A voice: "Take care. We've had a gas leak."

"We've had information…"

"One of our marines was caught

With his hands

In someone's black military silk drawers."

Though we now know there's a Soviet team checking

Out our installations in Poland

Where we send …But everybody knows black sites. (Who says? The NYT proposes 54 countries helping the CIA's secret detention and interrogation program…)

A one star general peaks through a concealed window

What else could be done with all those Jews!
                           Picasso paints "Guitar (for Stein.)" Cry
out: "Long Live Lenin, Stalin, MAO… Like Elia Kazin,

name names!" They
didn't.
"Has anyone ever slept in this room?"

"Colonel Cryptof. He was caught."
"Why?"
"Didn't translate correctly."

At the intersection of Cathedral and Paris, he was followed by 2 men in

Burberies, whistling the Third Man…
                     They catch
Up with him, shoot him in the neck.

"What a sorry way to go, don't you agree?

            You're his replacement."

            "Are you preparing my exit from this world?" "It's
an experiment."
"Please, lie down on your back. We'll demonstrate."
            He does.
            "Look! He's got an erection!!!" Elec-
tric wires tied around his chest.
            "Yell, if it hurts!!" "Oh!

Ouch!"
"More," says Solange.

Vomits.
Faints.
"Emily, cut off his dick

That'll make him stop asking all those ques-
tions." "Great! Always wanted to do just that!!!"
"Fill his mouth with Wonder Bread,
Ready him for his assignment."
Emily speaks into her Blue-
berry.

        Raymond Roussel writes: "Comment j'ai …"

A record plays Bing Crosby's X-mas
song. Lionel Hampton plays.
Gibberish.

"Give me Dizzy, any time!"
  He's released.
  "Had enough? Your mission is…"
  Piss

  Dribbles down the mattress.
  Nearly swallows his tongue.
  He whistles the International

Solange and Emily stand at attention. Whistle with him.
Scratchy nails on a blackboard.
　　　"Dancing in the Dark." Solange and Emily do so.

　　　"O! What fun it is to ride…"

　　　　　　　　　　　　　　　　　　　　　　　　　bullets?"
　　　　　　　　　　　　　Lenin says: "Did you hear a hail of

"…………………" Saint-Just says, in French:

Now, a Superman comic. Let him fly to his planet and get refueled.

　　　Solange picks up a long iron stick

"Is that what you've been looking for, Emily?" Blushes,
　　　　"Lie down on your pissy mattress."
　　　Blushes.
　　　"Ok? Do you want more?"

　　　Baudelaire writes: "Lesbos, terre des nuits chaudes et
　　　langoureuses…"

　　　"Sing along, if you wish."
　　　"O mayo!"

　　　Her stomach shrills. She gurgles: "Hold the tuna."
"It's all in de woids ain't it? Would you prefer a line from HOWL?"

She's hard of hearing. "Go on."

What a tough act to follow!

The speakerine says: "it's about time!!!"

"One day, maybe, I'll remember all of that

Memory stuff."

"Buy 2 tickets for the Orient Express."

Both will travel on that train…drink champagne and eat oysters.

"Ok for you?" He turns to the 2 women at
the station.
Repeats:
"OK for you?"

"In the cabin, I shall sleep in the upper berth, Emily and Solange

Below. That'll do after midnight. What a pleasure to hear you move

Around the couch making

Slight orgasmic noises! "

"Now, we're about to reach Bucharest. On the platform, as it is done

            On platforms all over France
"We'll get out, stroll, buy a ham and cheese in a baguette,with cor-
nichons, butter,

            Dijon mustard and red wine." The
            whistle blows.
"This Orient Express... if you did not know," he says to Solange and

 Emily: "In the beginning (Isn't it always: "in the beginning?")
 " Crossed the English Channel, heading for the Black Sea.
Some wish to baptize it the "Flying Scotsman."
Others, the "Twentieth Century Limited." (Neither
            was found acceptable.|
            "What you'll discover, in that most elegant train

            Through solid

     Gold doors, thirteen different ones... We
 shall pass through Germany, Austria
                 Czechoslovakia , Hungary and "Romania."

To add to the last stop, trust Agatha for further precisions. Once

Running back to

Our suite.: "I nearly forgot Athens and then Bulgaria and Istanbul. You

Shall see the

Ostend-Vienna."

George Oppen writes: "All things/Speak if they
speak…"

"Express links up with the Orient Express.
Then, when we get past

Budapest, we're in

Belgrade. I can …

Vouch for Belgrade, and that splendid 4 star Hotel. The front desk will

Give
Us
Passes

For the dining room and, if you're interested, three other passes

To a boxing match near the

Dining room. If

You're interested, the cars date back to six wheelers, with four-berth

TICKTICKTICKLIKELIKELIKE

sans dire…" Lighting by Benjamin Fondane writes: "Il va

old-fashioned German petroleum lamps. The
locomotives were the 2-4-O,
              With a double

              Frame.

 The Austrian models burnt brown coal and added a huge, basin-shaped top to their
Chimneys. " Solange coughs.
                    "Please, stop that guide book shit." Em-
                    ily dittos. "Are you an Orient Express
                    publicist?"
                    Both giggle,

                    Powder their noses.

              Their compartment door slides open.

              You can see middle-aged women powdering their noses

And dressed for tea time.

Elegant women, dressed for tea time, cheerfully lean on the bar and ap-
plaud the

                    Country Side.
                  Solange
            Turns towards Emily, not yet quite awake. "Let's make our
way to the restaurant." They push
                    By elegant middle-aged women, Well-
                    dressed
                    Long red dresses and men in tuxedos, with silky

          Folded handkerchiefs in

          Their lapels. Once

          There, the maître d' escorts them to their reserved table

Overlooking the green country

          Side and rarely a

Village with men and women working in the fields. " Oysters
For me only if it's an "r"

          Month, then I'll order

Oysters and a bottle of Beacaillou."
"Oysters for me, too."
The waiter hovers over us, writing down our desires…Solange adds:
"With dainty potatoes."

She adds: "Haven't you ever heard

Of a double conjugation: Sex and food? I'll also take a slice
of pinkish lamb with British

Mint on the side."

"Seen any good movies lately?" She sits next to me and
mumbles

Something about

How dangerous it may be for the three of us to witness a
murder on the

Ori-
ent Express. "I think, if You ask, I know the end,
because I think I know the dialog. I've

Memorized it. It's a silent memory trip, I mean
memory… You know, even when I

Close my eyes, I see memory, refueling, refusing to
enter! Please, close the compartment door."

"And you?" I ask in a round-about

Manner.

       She comes up

With the most unexpected question: "Did you ever see,
Before leaving New York,

       Boltansky's Major

Exhibit? If I think about it, I can imagine in those

Extermination camps

Prisoners undressing.
Clothing

Piled up on the platform.

They say he found them in New Jersey, not far from Man
Ray's hometown, in a recycled bin." Solange asks: "why
are we stopping?"
"There's a train up ahead. Perhaps they're filming a

New sequence?" She

Turns

Towards Agatha. "Not in my script," she says,

Affirmatively.

She suffers from arthritis,
Needs to walks up
And down the corridor.

Refuses Valium. She says: "when my

Grandmother lost her

Voice-- too much screaming-- she learned how to lip

Read.

Important for silent movies,

                         And that may

Explain some of the moving lips in silent films when

They say what they shouldn't. As of

That moment,
 grandma was paid when

A children's class sat in the front row of the Edison on

Columbus Avenue and 100 st.
Pop corn made
    Marcel Proust writes: "Indeed, I have forgotten

Who Madeleine was…"

A repetitive noise, then
A quasi-silent one. Kids
got up.
Fights broke out

Girls screamed when boys put their

Hands in the wrong… A
lady, next to me,
Wears an old-fashioned Chanel, says: "I
don't believe a word you say. My
Grand-daughter saw that same movie, and then, when

She got home, not a peep about boys."
(White hair
CONCEALED.)
Concealed her white
Tuff radiation spots, here and there. Radiation
spots here and there. Red shoes. Agatha says:
"Take all that down. It'll help me."

Solange and Emily look on, admiringly. The two hold

Hands playing

With their skin-tight Italian leather gloves.

"Tonight, I'll join you in the lower berth. Make sure

Your blanket is

Thrown aside."

"Was there anything else worth repeating? "

Cigarette smoke rises in the compartment, leaving traces on the window pane. Emily

Draws a

Heart. Solange

An arrow.
At that moment, the Orient Express leaps off the tracks.
"Would you care for a 30 yr old cognac, after dinner?" In

fact, as three policemen make it clearer, no Orient Express
has ever gone off its tracks.

"Perhaps, on the 11 o'clock

News, we'll learn that some terrorist gang planned it all
along." (On the radio, a flash flood named Jeepers...)

Agatha smiles, pencil in hand,
She thinks, we'll
Never identify the bodies, at least not until we reach

Istanbul.

"Damn it, I haven't finished my

Beaucaillou," Solange says, in her pinky-blue voice.
"Tough on me! I'll do it another day."

Somebody leans out,

Raises his voice, says, "Her hand-bag was thrown out
the window.
                              Is everything alright?"

She asks the Conductor.

TICKTICKTICKLIKELIKELIKE

    "Ask him what the hell's going on? Is it simply a question of temporality? After
all, from what we can make out,

        the locomotive has

                     "Dali…Dali…Dali…"

Turned into mangled steel.

Agatha leans in the corner. She's soon fast asleep. You

can hear her gently Breathing
through her nose. You can hear
her mumbling: "How I wish I had
written
"Murder on the Orient Express!"

"What a pleasure to shake hands with Lauren Bacall,
Ingrid Bergman and, if you ask me,

 Albert Finney,

But I can't remember anyone else. I've got a heavy
memory . If I could count, I'd say at least a 50 lbs.

Problem."

She turns around:
                  "Albert Finney." Then,

She dozes off. You can hear her regular breathing. Now, she
stares out the window. It's

Solange's turn, but she's

Tight all the way. She recites an old New York Times left
behind

In the both sex toilet.

"Wash your hands before leaving." Then, she says, in a
whisper: "Did

You know that adult American Indians have the highest
suicide rates, by far?" We

All thought that the train had inched forward, at least, for
a second.
                    Drops of Channel 18

Dropped near Emily's foot.

  Agatha's "Madame Bovary" followed. At that moment, the

                    Conductor steps in.

"Don't you worry, we'll soon be out of this movie!"
We're watching, as the police drag

Out the

Dying.   Others pinch their noses.

Overheard:" Try. Try again. At least a stutter of
memory."

"As for us, trucks are on the way! For the price of our

tickets,

we might

As well live through a real adventure! No doubt, we'll be
put up in a 4 star Hotel! I can imagine the press

Pressing on us!"

One says to the other: "Do you think we've got enough

For a couple of duly executed nightmares?" Now, ciga-
rette butts crushed on a Turkish rug.

 Sirens. Ambu-
lances.
"Would you ladies care for a flute of Bollinger '38? Or

some

Calvados, circa 1870? If not, can you come up with
another suggestion by breakfast time?" Solange

Throws out a question:

"That reminds me of a rotten newsreel, or, if you've
got a good memory, how about

A Jay Arthur Rank movie with a beautiful Asian
boy banging on a giant drum?"

                    TICKTICKTICKLIKELIKE
(Like student talk.)
    Nobody answers. Emily nibbles Solange's
ear. Outside, a compartment door slides open.
    Two shots of cortizon in her left…

            Christian Morgenstein writes: "I
almost feel alive although I'm no longer me."

"Why don't You try a month's physical therapy? Try a couple of weeks at the
chiropractor."

    Shots.
    Terror-
    ists.
    "No more bikinis, no more miniskirts, no more
    blues. Wipe off your bluish lipstick
    And, if you ask my

Opinion, cover your blueish nipples."

She interrupts. "Was it that way in a front line

Hospital outside Manila?"

"If you ask my opinion, I mean, about that Manila
hospital,

Really, I was never there, but friends of mine took

Pictures of a couple of operations, Including
all that flowing blood drizzling Down on the
tiles."
"All that blood…"

"It's

Beginning to smell like an unwashed kitchen floor, with lots
of saw dust all around and,

If I can remember correctly, when a steak fell

On the dusty kitchen floor (was it in Paris?)
The waiter cleaned it up with his hands." "Don't you think it might be
A good shot to…

Picture our present state of being? "

"Now, I'd like a flute of Veuve Cliquot! How I
Wonder, how they are?"
We look from the outside.

"Let me interrupt. About my first husband, The
one who left
Me for that fuckin' Swedish maid. "

"Nothing like erasing the recent past! I don't want to
remember anything, but to no

Avail!!"

He quickly found one who had mothered three kids.

(A sergeant hums: " I'm dreaming of a black Christmas…")
She wanted three more,
More! So, my previous husband left her High and Dry!! But
he did leave her lots of sperm! Lucky the one to be Impreg-
nated.
Perhaps grow a Clark Gable mustache or Betty Grable's

blonde hair!

Decent of him, dontcha think? In any

Case, to

Hide his medals! Or just his sperm?"
Perhaps you
Spoke a different language?

I bumped into him in Rome. He wore a Poplin suit. I
Heard a woman cry out: "Poplin!"
He turned around. "I could have sworn I was staring at myself in a store

Window."

"Well, what about

You?"

"Same. I fell in love with Jody. We lived close by the RR Station
where, every

Sunday, cleaning women from the Philippines complained, ate tiny
sandwiches, sipped

Capucinnos with excessive amounts of sugar.

Jody and me, we lived it up, kissing from six in the morning

to

Six at
night night." She had
been a
Painter in Paris, living with a Romanian painter up in

Montmartre, as they used to do at

The turn of the century. A portrait painter of women's re-
laxed bodies as they got out of the bathtub and

Wrapped
themselves

In large
white towels.

She said she wanted a baby girl she could

Walk to school

Carry her lunch-box,

Then walk her over to the swimming pool on Leclerc.

Both were

Crushed by a

Drunken driver near rue Daguerre. She
died within minutes, too late
For an

Ambulance.

"How we dreamt of spending our honeymoon off the

Purple Grotto

Near the Purple Grotto!"

"Were you talking Serbo-Croatian with a Montenegro ac-
cent?"

"How about we

Discuss, this once, I mean the Orient Express, when it
reaches Constantinople? Can't Wait..."

She says: "May

I, (in parenthesis) complain about that bearded con-
ductor, always passing by, staring at...

What everybody
Was wearing. If I had my wish, I'd cut off his balls in the
Kitchen!! In the "where," can't remember. Leave me

alone. "

In the meantime, to quote a Soviet leader, "What's to be
done?" " Let me remind you that, if

We like to fuck

Don't mean we'd be a happily married couple! Can't you
hear gun shots?

Duck. Hear the

Loudspeaker: "This

Is your chief engineer, we're being fired upon by un-
known assailants. Until

Further notice, do not leave your compartment. Let
me add, stay away from your
Windows."

TICKTICKTICKLIKELIKELIKE

Could it be the sound

Of fingers dribbling on an old Beckstein, a few

Cars up ahead?

Now a bushel of Screams.
Again, unidentified noises, Unidentified sounds.
"Help! Help!" Then a fearful silence.

Once again, the loudspeaker: "Women, line up in the corridors."

"If Poirot doesn't work out, I'll call in Holmes and his doting Watson.

Let's not give up

All hope..."

Solange and Emily chime in. "In all cases, let's not jump to conclusions."

One after the

Other, women

Dribble down the 39 steps. The
first one is shot dead.
The second one cringes.

Keyserling writes: "le 'moi' de l'homme ou de la femme...est indépendant du temps" Then adds : "L'homme ne devient en réalité ce qu'il souhaite devenir... "

A stubby Stooge

Pushes women down the steps.

The third is ordered to run for her life just like… Now, in
a whisper: "You can hear the near silence of

flying   drones. Ours

                              Head-
quartered in

West   Hurley   Not
far   from   Wood-
stock."

Drones hover above for 18 hrs. Even more secretly than ever
before (our healthy) unmanned.

"To keep you abreast: the U.S. has more than 7000 to its
credit,

More if you count those on our coastal ships."

(Voice off) Between 282 or 533 civilians reported killed,
including women and kids. All terrorists. Jihadists.

Special Forces took over a deserted high school parking lot in West

Hurley.

 Parked a fleet of their own yellow school buses in the back
yard.

Even more secretive, those

Buses have sophisticated dials implanted in their dash-
boards.

They can check out every

Danger spots

Over the Whole Wide World,

This time, within reach of three farm houses, Up
ahead, toward the east. A
Clear voice over a bullhorn: "If you wish to recover your

loved ones, please do so within

The next 30 minutes and deposit them

In the last car of the Orient Express.

You'll find them in the High Grass."

A few of us

Run out and recover bodies,

Grab as many as we could, pushed them inside the

Open doors of the last car.

The train turned into a cemetery.

We rush out. The heaviness of the smell is

Unbearable. As

We proceeded, the conductor comes out of our im-
peccable toilet. We

Believe someone had flushed down a musical score.

Suddenly, eight ballerinas skip around.

practiced

Four wore tu-tus, worked on their entre-chat.
Four others

Their pas (PERDUS) de chat Jeté.

Earlier, all legs had been stretched on the bar, below the windows.

This justified their presence. One said to the

Others: "Let's get the conductor."

They rip off the grey line, used to stop the train. Fol-
lowed the

Conductor. Took Him to the dining room.

Told him to remove his belt. Held
him down with the line on
The grey-white linen table cloth, stitched with a green and
white snowy scene

Of a mountain village. A
ballerina
Holds up a hand-stitched red flag:

THE PRAVDA BELARUS DANCE COMPANY Went to the kitchen
Found an electric

Cutting utensil.

Still quiet, they show him the knife. Point
to his waist. "There,"
She said and,

With a single straight gesture, cut his body in half. To
celebrate, they opened the fridge and
Gulped down large plastic bottles of Diet Coke.

All this was recorded in the second yellow school bus.
"Colonel,

What's to be done?" Frank Sinatra's voice was meant to
quiet them down.

It didn't.

They drove down Clover Street or some name or other.
Turned right on Willow.
Colonel Ames sat next to his

 PFC driver.

All of a sudden, the

Engine dies. Ames

leaps out.
"What the hell's going on?" This said in a stentorian

voice. "How long Will
this charade Last?"
A woman steps out of her black Dodge 4X4,

Wearing

Gold pointed heels.

"Let me tell you a story, if I can remember it correctly.

When I graduated West Point,

I saw her.
I asked her to marry me. She came from a

Very comfortable family with a

Horse farm in Maryland and the top floor of 15, Central

Park West.

She loved horses, collected English bridles.

Had a

Personal trainer, an iconic specialist in dressage from

Germany.

"In dressage" I said undervoiced.

"She loved cars. Lots of horse power.

Asked her building contractor to build her a huge garage. In it, she drove in a 1930

Hispano Suiza, a 1976 Lamborghini counter back LP 400, more "I said to myself a Lamborghini 350 TV (1932) and a Countach and…a 1936 Bugatti, type 57 Atalante."

"Anything else?"

'Yes. A Bufori she ordered from the Kuchar brothers
located in Kuala Lampour.
(She was so rich, she said to herself, she could have the car
outfitted in silver just like in a Great Gatsby movie.)

"I think I had a dream.

I saw myself walking down a dark corridor,
Could it be an advanced image of the unconscious at the end of a Black
Door? I

My father opened it. Inside, I hoped to find my shadow memory.

Never hugged me.

He never held me in his arms.

Never kissed me. He

Did wash his hands.

Flushed the toilet when he pissed.

I couldn't I call him dad, as my 7th
            graders did.

Then, I wrote my first poem: Pity me
            Hopeless We're a
pair
            Memory and me.

By whose lips does memory speak? An
echo?
If I knew, everything would be audible, I'd be

Overwhelmed by choices Deco-
rated, or as a standby? A forecast?

A consolation? Voluptious, at least. As a
mendicant, I undressed.
I felt as if I were my own black box. I did everything above,
without drugs!

As of now, I shall never be

Overpowered by a dismissal

Now, over the past Now,
I can no longer Reject my
shadow

Me, when I was without a
"was." Now, I
Call him "dad."
Shadow boxing.
I say, there's a run on

Poetry! Here's mine:

Was it a narrative? A repulsion? Groddeck
writes: "this is not a prose poem."
When I *was very young,* old
enough to remember Remem-
bered others, was it
Myself?

writes: "

Italo Svevo

                In fact, Making
        her
                  Live my life."

Walter Scott's "Kenilworth":

                "You should travel backwards..." Did
                I forget
                    Anything else?

                        YES!

                                    Orwell's

"Such, such were

                The joys."

Now,

                I've drained my haystack.

Transmutated a

"Now"

"Colonel, your PFC wrote a

Poem:

"Once Upon a Time..."
That's mine:
    Posthumous lines... a breach of

Human entities.

Once

I thought I knew my mirror

In blank verse

In time: chacun son goût!"

He knew he had

Sea-calf's eyes

Thrown away
Knowledge and on
Whose behalf
I've driven past my shadow."

"Nuts:" as Benjamin Fondane says:

"You're driving me Nuts." He
did say that. By now,
Three other stretched limos,

On one, a thule on the roof, anchored to the right.
"When will
You move your fuckin' bus out of the way?" she
screamed : Vulgar for once.
'We're in a hurry. Our friends are waiting for us at

The cemetery." She

Begins to cry. Ames takes out a military handkerchief

Gives it to her. A mechanic

Insists: "We'll get

This shitty bus out of her way. You'll soon be…"

The colonel excuses the delay. "There's something in the
back of my mind." You've got a

Beautiful Schumacher Buick."

You said: "keep your mind off the delay. Let me Tell
you a story, something I can string together."
                              "Please."
 "Many times ago

Can't be more precise.

 When I graduated West Point, at a lavish

Banquet,

I asked her to marry me." "That
fast?"
"If I could only activate my past…"

She came from a very comfortable family, with a horse farm
in Maryland and a fancy

Penthouse at 15, Central Park West. You could not be

Richer: $64.000 a year in Federal taxes. She
said: "build me a huge…"
I heard that one before. (Was my memory ticking?) As a
matter of hearing, didn't you
Name those priceless cars?

She remembered buying: "Guess what's in my thule…."
(She remembers buying 3 30 lb bags of ice.)

She repeats, still crying, "You see my Dodge 4x4?

I've made it into a double. I bought 3 packs of ice in 30 lb
bags. You know why…

I won't tell you what's in my thule. You
guess.
You'll understand. My two kids were killed by an
oncoming train. My two kids

Were killed by an oncoming train. Both were much too
close to the rails. When

The barriers

Came down,
they ran across, or so they thought. The train came.

Couldn't stop. Fritsi died on the spot and so did…"
"Please don't cry. I feel for you. My
Two kids also died

In a terrible accident, too close to an airplane taking off, near
the base, close to our

Home. You know,

From my uniform, I'm a colonel. That I'm a colonel."
"So's my Ex."
The

Dodge had been turned into a hearse, An
AC hearse.

"Don't ask what's in my thule. My dearest
friends, in the other two limos,

Thinking it was fall, turned off

Their ac.

We arranged everything by e-mail. My friends thought it
was an

Indian summer and

Turned back the ac. You could hear it murmur. The
lady choked.
"My kids…" He thinks he remembers saying: "if

　　　You go to a summer private school program in Spain to
brush up on your Spanish,

careful."

Be careful. There're lots of dealers around. Be

　　　Then I think about all our wonderful,

　　　Wonderful talks when I said

　　　To my baby-sitting daughter

　　　"Have someone drive you home. If you still want to get into

Wood's Hall, be sure

　　　To work on your math,

　　　On your math," I repeated. "Just because you know how to
write, that's not good enough. I

　　　Promise you, if

You, if you do get

Accepted, I'll buy you a blue blazer, 3 regimental khakis, and ten button-down whites

And the same in

Blue,
Loafers, tennis shoes, dancing shoes and walking shoes." And I added: "Be extra careful in school, and especially after

school, when you go to

The park to play

Soccer... Be extra careful! You never know if there isn't a weirdo checking you out.

Remember, your soccer

Shorts are really short!

quite revealing! Mother

Remember, your team shirt is...well,

Says come home

When you finish the game."

"We're about to go!" Says

The PFC driver. Ames hops in.

Waves good-bye to the woman. "Hope You'll
not be too late for your funeral." The yellow
bus turns right on H24.

Woodstock up ahead. Orders

Flash on:

Foucault writes: "There is…no absolute
right and wrong in love…"

The yellow dial.

"Send three drones over the stalled Orient

Express.

Aim at:

Freud writes: "Let's check out your memory... (like a pulse.)"
Three groups of
Terrorists, ten meters away from the train, to the left. "Colo-
nel Ames, we're
Counting on

You."

Not a peep out of the bus. All fully armed. Pass the cemetery,
heading

Toward

(Ludwig Wittgenstein writes: "Can a hu-
man body feel pain?")

Woodstock: "Good for the morale."

The driver and his men had spent too much time

Enclosed in their

Yellow buses, parked in the school parking lot.

Looked around. Saw a multitude of tourist stores and a pastry shop.
Perfect place for
X-Mas shopping. A Pain Poilane in the window: "all for us!" The

colonel, in

A clear voice,

Orders the first bus to order a drone to clear out that farm house up

Ahead where

He suspects the enemy
was holding out. A concealed Silence.
The second bus stalls. A Mechanic
has the know-how, Lifts up the
hood.
Fiddles around. Says,

"OK. Now, you can go!" No-
 body cared.
"Had our MQ IC Gray eagle drone wiped out the enemy?"
"Colonel Ames, Congratulations! You've just wiped out a good part of
one of those farm houses. As we can judge, all were killed!" He reflects a
second.
               Memorized the following: "Colonel

Ames, with that victory, you've earned a Gold

Medal to be pinned on your left lapel, the day you come home! Think of

At least three TV interviews!"

Adds:" Were there civilians, I mean, Innocent bystanders? Isn't that's

Tough! Women and Animals?   Children picnicking? We could check out
terrorists with

Their latest combat AKA's, hiding in the High Grass, not far from the

Orient Express."

In a few months, snow will cover the remains of the third farm house. "As
  you know, nobody hears drones approaching! What a
                              Happy

  Great silence, don't you think? As we say at HQ, 'whooptydoo'!
We're

  Three Cheers ahead of anyone else!" Soldiers, around Colonel Ames,
  Praise the success of our
  Batwinged RQ 170 sentinel drone! The men yell out: "Long Live our
  Drones! The next act will be the destruction of the 2nd farm! We've
caught sight of three terrorists, hiding behind a family of 5.

                    Collateral damage?
Well, one of

Our drones, yet another, with an excellent memory, probably going back to his adolescent

Thrills, praised Lockeed Martin, says, without that company 's
intelligence and, if I can remember,

Due to Nazi scientists we grabbed in Berlin in 1945, this might not

Have been such a success! No drones would have existed not meaning to
kill an
Innocent, beardless young American Peace Corp boy, teaching farmers how
to plant in winter."

"Well, Colonel, can you imagine a plethora of letters to the New York

Times!!" In the…"

meantime, hundreds of college students, all around the country, on their
campuses,

Prepared a huge march on CIA HQ.

(Did they ever suspect Central Command was located in the

Pentagon? And, C.I.A. below the cemetery?) Did they ever suspect it was
concealed under

(TICKTICKTICKLIKELIKELIKE)

Arlington Cemetery?

The Cherry Orchard

Heidegger writes: "But father, open-eyed, let me meet at last your face."

I stared at myself in the mirror on the wall, and I asked if my muted face, asked who I was.

Said: "I'm sick to my stomach." I couldn't look at him. I try holding his hand. Sweaty. Other people came into the room. Some brought candy, Others, flowers. They hugged.

Nurses come and go
Eye wobbly jell o

My face is still covered with shaving cream. Handsome Italian young men twirl their car keys, standing on the sidewalk, checking out babes across the street. Light cigarettes. Crush them on the sidewalk.

Remembers a mattress. A girl wearing red on her naked

body. "Come in," she says. I hear the fat young lady saying. "Ok! Which one..? " I point to the red one. "That one," I say. In that tight room, a ceiling mirror. I see her on the bed, FLAT ON HER BACK. She had razored under her arm. Her pubs. She asked for lots of extras. I said I never knew any of that. "I'll show you." Like a kindergarten teacher, she said lots of things. I followed her instructions: rubbing, biting, plunging, shivering, convulsing. Three years of German and I could read and recite Hölderlin. Or had I thought I had memorizes it?

I asked myself if I did really exist or did all this depend on an image of myself flashing back? Who then is looking at me?

He could smell the rolling food tray on its way. Three open graves nearby.

A nurse called at 7:30.

Like)
In the distance, Big Ben ticked away. His add for death.

TICKTICKTICKLIKELIKELIKE

"I'm so sorry, your father died at 3:15 this morning. His breakfast tray, with its yellow feet, dropped to the floor, scrambling his corn flakes.

He repeated, ten times, at least: "Mary," or was it "Mosey?" And then he clasped his hands as if he were

Saying hello or good-by to a friend. He babbled. I think he was delirious. I believe he was having Hallucinations. It was exactly 3:12. My ear close to his mouth."

"

James Joyce writes:" I don't care a flaming damn what anyone called him…"

He seemed surrounded by unacknowledged memories: faces, hands, voices. (I mumbled: "was I the son, a duplicate of

Myself?") The cleaning woman found a piece of paper under the left side of the bed and, scratched on it:

"Son."

Avishai Margalit writes: "whether we are under a moral obligation to remember (or to forget)?"

Same writer: "memory is built upon a network ..."

 Your father wrote: "Son, here's a brief network of thought:

        Inhibitor like silence in a crowd
        Homophonic intervention Remember
        our..."
        I keep on wondering, in my state, at this time,

        How my memory could have escaped seclusion? Or,
had it been, partially, at least, founded on a non-working network,

        Hidden like an afikomen hid-
        ing memories?

(Mary or Mosey was my mother's name.)

James Joyce writes: Your mother must have gone through a good deal of suf-
fering," then he added: "Whatever else is unsure in this stinking dunghill
of a world, a mother's love is not."

Father used to play.

My mother had nearly forgotten her German.

The silence of love

Was it a form of a puritanical hesitation? An
emotional prudence?
We hardly ever kissed, even after my graduation.

In the Song of Solomon: "There is no flaw in you."

Pannetone.

As a family, it seemed to me we were like raisins in a

A constellation?

Ann Lauterbach writes: "There was the shield of another language. " Did
she know we had a hearing voice?
                    Marina Tzvetaieva writes: "Je suis heureuse de vivre de

façon simple et exemplaire."

Women wore black hats with matching shawls.
There was never any grief.
                    Minor, her maiden name.

          Father sat at the head of the table

          Words escaping.

          I never drank hot milk, not even when I was a baby in
Paris. I hated that skin floating on top.

          It was only after her death that we found a huge,
well-stacked yellow- lined paper where my mother had jotted down her
impressions of her Paris Bar colleagues, friends, and her life.

          In the meantime, Father recited, by heart, The
          first ten pages of War and Peace.
Colonel Ames' voice: "Reason"… tells his men, over a loudspeaker,

connecting the three yellow buses—

"Remember men, next week we'll be Elsewhere. (Did
you ever imagine story-telling as a carousel:
"All sizes, all colors, all riders, all horses, arms stretched, trying to snap up
the magical ring? Out of all those repetitive rounds, in a circular distance:
the ring and a free ride.")

 "I don't know about you guys but, do me a favor, please, don't commit sui-
cide: There have been, according to the latest info, 22 a day in the military.
(Death enveloped thought as if not a single breath had been allowed to be.)

When I was young, I thought the sky was a blank piece of paper, then…a huge thunderstorm rent the Sky in half. I was able to patch up the sky and make it whole, once again, or so I thought.

I hardly knew my father. When I was 8, he held me in his arms (so rare an event!) and began opening the door to his

Past, stopping at times, whispering, as if, what he was trying to remember was so

painful, he had to stop. Then he would whisper, said he had a wounded memory in college. He sat around the bar, at the West End, laughing at the moving circular series of jokes above.

A Columbia assistant prof.

thinking he was part of the group, laughed when they did. One of the silent jokes above, had a Shark swallowing a man's head.

He spoke how Johnny had studied the origins of language as a possible Indo-European source of law. How Language fortified class distinctions, how, in fact, language was at The Bottom of all Social and Economic Infra-Structures. He was a vociferous reader of the works of Linguists, Anthropologists, Archeologists. After having digested all those sources of intellectual nourishment, he concluded, with a smile, that, in his opinion, one had to shout:

"Languages of the World Unite." Dad

had a radical touch.

Kerensky and

Minor.

HE: "MINOR? Isn't that your name? Isn't? HE:
"Who's Minor?
HE:" Are you hard of hearing memory? HE:"
OK. I...
HE: "MOVE ON. He:
"I can't.
HE: "What's in your mouth?

HE:"I guess, food...

HE: " Good....What kind of food?
HE:" I can't say... HE:"
Chins?   Or...   HE:"
More...
HE:" Something like that. Maybe...
HE:" Maybe tongues...
HE:" Tongues. He:"
Maybe... HE:" Move
on. HE:" Maybe...
HE: Siberia?
HE:" Is this a police interrogation...?

HE:" Now... you find yourself in a filthy police station.
 HE:" Windows shielded by filth.
HE:" Did they ask you a thousand questions?

HE:" Can't remember. HE:"
CAN'T? Or Won't?
HE:" I lived in filth. Tikhon and Bezsonov let themselves die.
HE:" Anything else in your head?
HE:"A dark prison. Somebody screamed. HE:"
Did you give them anything?

HE:" No.!...

HE:" February 2, 1888.... HE:"
Now, we're moving!
HE:" Narodnai Volia, founded in 1884.

HE:" What's that? HE:"
...

                  We began singing. I can sing it for you. He:"
Do it.
HE: "You've been cut down...

HE: "Anything else comes to mind? HE:"
 No.
HE:" Siberia?

HE:" Clouds of insects...I couldn't escape the ears, the noses, the eyes, the mouths...

HE:" You see!! There goes your mouth! HE:"
NIGHTS GOT DARKER.

HE:" Go on. More...

HE:" Tesselkin. Kharitonoff......

HE:" Minor...Somebody's calling you.

HE:" Only 22 were still alive. We nearly froze to death.
HE:" More...

HE:"At night, we talked Marx, Lenin, Rousseau. The history of Russian

Tyranny.

HE:" What a memory… Who's talking about lapses?

HE:"I heard a friend's sharp intake of breath. Guards came in and hit him, with the butt of their rifles.

HE:" How can I thank you enough for your remembrances!

ADDITION

OTHER (artificial) MEMORIES

SHE:" Did you know Minor?

SHE:" No.

SHE:" Your senior graduation book and school records include a pho-tograph of you two dancing the jitterbug in the pre-graduation April auditorium.

She:" Must have been a mistake. Anyway, no.

SHE:" What were your favorite readings in your sophomore year?

SHE:" Can't recall.

SHE:" Were you an ardent lesbian/feminist in class discussions?

SHE:" Can't recall.

She: "Can you explain, as a senior art history major, why there were so

few women painters before the 20th century? SHE:

"You got me!
SHE:" Wasn't your favorite bedtime reading: "Women in DADA"?
Like Suzanne Duchamp, Gabrielle Buffet-Picabia, Beatrice Wood,
or painter-collagists like Miss Kurt Schwitters, Man Ray's sister, or
Hannah Hoch... or Sophie Taeuber...

SHE:" Stop! I can't stand lists...

SHE:" What about EVIL (put this in CAPS), I mean Eve (Ning)? I...
SHE:" If ever someone were to ask you who were his...Question:
uouze descendants?"

SHE: "I'm ...can't do it. I mean, what can't I say.

           Antonin Artaud wres:"............................
....
....
..............0.........

....
....

....
..........................VOILA JUSTEMENT..."

          AND
          AGAIN:

SHE: "At the very least, are you not capable of coming out with an answer?

SHE:" Do you really want me to invent mimickry?
SHE:" Did you ever play a Picasso's guitar?

SHE adds:" Whose
your favorite actor or actress?

SHE:" The list is as long as those cars parked up ahead.

"Then, switch to the Berlin Wall.

Why had Moscow built it?"

He caught sight of a plasticized woman singing the Third International.

A simple question rose up in his mind.

Would you have done anything

To save your life?

Now, a chorus of bullets.

Dad stopped. He wanted to unite

Lines.

Past and Present, Eliminate Faults

Dad used to say we all had a moral conscience (like card- car-rying Existentialists.)

He stopped, as if words had flown out of his mental coup. He lived in parentheses.

The near absence of words.

Horrors in the world.

A past unencumbered …unencumbered… There… Or
was it a built-in painted memory?

Dad said, that moment, when parts of his memory snapped into…

a blank place…

He dodged the page.
What's the point of mirroring absence?

Everything existed, sidelined like actors in the wings of…

What if it said the world was a coffee ice-cream cone, dripping on the left
side?

Now, a flag folded, handed over to the weeping widow.

I still can't call him dad…

A figure of speech.

TICKTICKTICKLIKELIKELIKE the
world…

I didn't even suspect such questions could

Arise. I said: "did

You know memory embellishes the present, especially if there's… Or
could it be that memory is a joke?"

(Kids laugh.)

I tell myself, if inside the word there isn't another one filling up that space
without our

Knowing it? Will it bypass our censors? I'd like to alienate…

"let it be, let it be…"

How I scorn amnesia, but I can't escape it, I mean,

This recurrence of an imagined past, like a backstage rehearsal for
meaning, and then,

Afterwards, the curtain would rise and dreams would step forward, Take
a bow, then, all of them,

In their sweaty costumes, would disappear into the next show. A

rehearsal

Always gives way to another one in the darkest of nights, like... but who can come up with a missing word?

At that moment, my only pleasure would have been to check out my dream, and photograph it,

Smelling, or still, like scowling dead bodies! You can tell on their faces... Now, only muted witnesses.

Could they ever be as accurate as a surreal pipe dream? But then

A thought, a picture of a thought- dreams.

A supplementary reality or, at best, an oversized poster

Stretched out on 42nd street.

No money could buy that dream!

Only a malaise remained, awakening me. It all comes down to Log Cabins or Camembert.

You might as well say a cabin model or,

Camembert.

You might as

Well, say

A provocation.

.All that checked out.

Universities, with lots of tenured Profs. living

 in buildings, overlooking Riverside Drive and that, over the past hundred years.

"Too often," one said, "we're tempted to

Erase repetition from our mind's brain, as a cored memory as if, indeed, our

Memory could not even reflect a disguise.

only real competitor

Was the Realist discourse."

Can you remember, if that's not a lie?

Colin Crisp writes: "It's

Meanwhile, Clementine, a junior high school student, fell

In love

With Jerry. (Both had read "Venus in Fur," and, on page 275 of the

French edition:

"Bonzes, Bramines, Imans, militaries, cadis, hommes de toutes

nations, de tout

Genre, de tout âge, rien n'était rebuté." (How
happy she was

After having read the Quote quoted above...)

They slept together,

tongue tied. They went swimming. She
wore a Blue bikini.

Clementine went to Barnard in NY.

He got a basketball scholarship to Penn State, and got it all with free

tuition.

The following Easter vacation, they

Bumped into each other in Grand Central Station, thinking nothing had

Changed.

        (How wrong they were!) They
found a cheap hotel in the East Village, east of
Tompkins Park. In the middle of the night,

Clementine got up.

She had lowered her see-
Through cotton panties.

On her way back, half-asleep, she

Stopped in the kitchen, borrowed a fork and went back where

Jerry was sleeping.

        She forked him to death.

        "Such a tragic story," said an op. ed.
in the NY Times.

(But a great rehearsal for

picking up a slice of a Thanksgiving turkey
wing.)

Wrote

"Can't all forks be outlawed?" Wrote an editorial in the Nation.

The Police found a big glob of blood on such a pleasant night. "Why?"

In the near distance, nights flashing, probably a street lamp

Awakened.

Or heavy rock music.

Stars ignored what had just happened. A police van drove up to the house.

A gurney rolled out like an airport

conveyor belt.

The body, wrapped in a dirty, torn sheet. People
stood around. "did

You ever see a corpse?"

morgues!"

"I saw a famous photographer who found pleasure in "Why do you think we're standing here?" She asked. "I forget my Leica."

"So close to IKEA?"

At noon, the smell of lentil soup cooked with

A slice of a dried tomato and slices of white onions.

Babies crying, a college graduate mother switched off the light. She

Sang a childish ditty,

Pushed a bottle of lukewarm milk

Into her newborn.

Changed her diapers, angled them into the kitchen garbage.

Smoked a filtered cigarette.

On the rug, a furry baby rabbit.

Looked… Like.

Mother says: "can't you hear a baby clock ticking
away?"

"Now, pick up

Your weapons. Open fire when you hear my orders." As

Day broke, in a split second, we fired an alliteration: Bullets came fast and furious.

Passengers

Able to walk, looked back on the Orient Express, locked in time.
Across the country side.

Two hour later, in Paris, Le Monde printed the names of the dead, close to

A dead body from Lindenhurst, seduced by the

Orient Express.

A Junior State Department official was sent to recover American bodies and help them

Fly home for a decent burial.

A postcard, with half an address, meant to reach Molly Berkowitz, 12 Travel

Rd. Lindenhurst. The junior

Rep. read it: "Dear Molly, I'll show you the most exciting pictures when I get back.

Your Dear

Friend, Rachel."

Others sat in the shade. Some talked about Professor

Bloom's interpretation of the Bible, Shakespeare, and a contemporary

American poet. How
would

Umberto Eco interprete that postcard? When Junior returned to

Washington, he discussed what he had read.

"I was always the first one on the scene." I said that without providing any further info. I fell asleep. I told her that I had

Seen a Gucci hand bag in Rome, near an historic monument. I told her I had opened her purse to read her identity card. "Young man, do you know where she lived?"

He replied: "let alexandrines do the job:

I lived a long and tedious life where I travelled

Nobody cared for my wounds not even POPLIN. (If that was
really his name!)

"Ok?"

Let the body be on view in the Cheney High School auditorium. If you can
identify it, we'll give you a year's worth of

Sweet Gender

Colonel Ames looked around. He said, to his courageous men, "he'd give
them a party in a

Local beer joint, when all of this was
over." The men applauded in both buses.

However, he added, "we've got to mop up the area. A sky-born photo,

from one of our drones, would perhaps be a tricky thing

To explain: why 10 children had been killed, and that eighteen year old

American Peace corps boy."

Now you

Could hear heavy artillery.

Cries for help.

Colonel Ames hit the dashboard: "We've still

got time to gather up our dead. Remember,

remove their dog

Tags, and push them in between their two front teeth." "Help,
Help me, please…"

One of our passengers

Crawled on the ground.

Men leapt off the train. Blood on her face. At that very

Moment, as if choreographed, huge trucks wended their way towards The
Orient Express.

A barrage of machine gun fire.

"Was that a way of saving us"?

They could hear another loudspeaker, a used-up voice.

Agatha began tuning up an old fashion Fairy Tale:

"Once upon a time…"

Her publisher wrote her a letter: "Your ms doesn't fit the vocabulary

rules for 7

To 8 year old. Good luck. Try another Publisher. Imagine Woody Allen buy-
ing your book for his

Daughter,

even if it had perfect color photographs.".

A recent convert to Islam, quoted 2 Suras. Another quoted Quor. 40.71: "In
the

Boiling water then they shall be Burned'an, "When the clamps of iron

Shall be round their necks, chains:

They shall be dragged along.

       The fire."

"Now, 40.72: "In boiling Water then they shall be burned in the fire

When the new Conductor came on board, Solange, in a quiet voice, said: "I'll get an electric knife just like the

One we use for our Thanksgiving dinner." The same scene had been played, way back.

They agreed: "You Must Remember This…" But then, to keep up with the present, his stomach was severed in half.

Music disappeared in the near distance.

Blood reddened the table cloth. But, then again, the ms had been finished. Imagine Clementine in a

Private School on the Upper East Side. A promising student and a fine La

Cross player who played opposite

Mt. Sinai. You could see a crowd waiting for the cross town bus. Her parents had purchased a co-

Op so that Clementine could walk to school, all by herself. A few years later, she wasn't even 14, she fell in love.

Emmanuel Levinas writes: "Une raison qui s'ignore ou s'oublie… «

She too had read: "Madame Bovary." She too wanted lots of Paris.

Hector, what a Greek! He was the Chosen One. That year's Lover. Hector, the school champion Ping

       Pong

player often took a couple of days off to travel to a college competition. She quoted Edgar

Allen Poe: "And they loved with a love…" Everybody knew what was to fol-
low, between Poe and

Mallarmé.

They kissed a number of times on the back staircase. The first year, her
parents took her to

Antigua on a Delta flight. Who could forget it? Who could have guessed it?
Colonel Ames got up, folded his

pyjamas, opened the bathroom door, saw himself in that rectangular mir-
ror, the shape of the door.

(In fact, he couldn't admit it, but his body reminded him of his body.)

Brushed his teeth. Put the arrow on his medical scale: 140 lbs. Ok. Broad
shoulders. Sucked in

His stomach. Still, too much rice. Martinis. No more cookies or chocolates.

Jumped into the

Shower. He could smell the soap on his newly pressed colonel's shirt, lapping over the chair. Scratched

His head. Rested.

Let the bath water DROOL DOWN. Too much smoking, too much of an effort. His 2 kids

Kdded him, reminding him of an Eminent Danger.
They saw it on TV.

He knew it.

He must watch over his Men. He hears CIA telling him Drones are on the way. "Did we dispose of the kids?" He heard and

Replied: "Makes me sick." His face covered with shaving cream. A three- day old beard. He

Knew it was fashionable in Italy, where young men twirled their car keys, checking out the action on the

Other sidewalk. He remembered his midnight visit to a whore house in

Newburg. A huge mirror. Girls

Lounging around on a red sofa. A Waiting, Tough Lady. "What'll it be?" She asked in a northern accent.

"That one:" I said. "Follow me." She said. We slipped into a room no bigger than a closet with a tiny

(Clark Coolidge writes:" Use mirrors for ceilings.")

Mattress and a full size ceiling mirror. She undressed. I saw her nipples hardening.

Shaved pubs.

I caressed her back. She insisted on a few additional pleasures.

"Well," I said, "Show!!" She so indicated, and I tried to follow through where I could. I felt as if I were working out in a home porn movie. He heard a recording. He

Had been assigned to Germany because of his three year college course. He had gotten to the point...

He loved TV programs,

hated commercials. He timed them: 4 min. and a couple of spits. He muted them. When he saw a re-run, he could predict what the hell was going to happen. That, too, was a Source of pleasure. But what made him particularly happy was a day when the Sergeant asked if he had

Permission to blind fold his colonel. "There's a surprise for you!" He walked into his make shift Quonset.

Somebody famous once wrote: "Let there be light."

"Now, open your eyes!" He did, and saw a long rectangular table with lots and lots of watches, one next

To the other.

"Pick one."

Colonel Ames admired all of them, but especially the ones with black dials:

a Bocca,

a Titanium, a
Hublot,

a Tissot,

a calibre de Cartier Fortis, a
Lacoste,

a Dior.

A Rolex 1831, Platinum Day-Date with a Stella dial and a stunning bracelet

And a great number of others . But he didn't want to admit it, that Rose gold, beautiful Ultra-thin, automatic movement, Parmigiani Tonda, 1950.

TICK TICK TICKLIKELIKELIKE

(Did the ticking announce his forthcoming death?)

(Have you ever crossed Broadway and 86th street? After the green light, the light of LIFE, a red hand menaces you, the sign of DEATH, and numbers follow, one after the other, a second or

so apart.

Time to breathe?

(An advanced notice of a Long Island funeral?)

In the absence of recollections, of what he truly loved, he should ' a checked out the NY Times, December 16th 2012, p.A23. There, he would have literally creamed with joy, as he saw and pictured them to himself:

A Movado with black aluminium tachy meter bezel (one thousand, four hundred and 95 cents.)

A Tommy Hilfiger 18 carrots, Swiss made

A Cartier (the same set-up as above.) Clark

Coolidge writes: "A single small clock

In the shape of a pinkish cathedral…"

But, to his so pleasuable astonishment, he saw an ad for the Gucci 18 KT Gold watch
where the

black dial truly held center stage. He mused: "what about a Dior VIII or, lastly (for now!) the Harry Winston,

all

white dial!

(Col. Ames, self-hushed, sought a partial answer to his passion for watches, Passion, in the sense of Christ's. He knew that passion meant suffering or, at least to know, he transferred that word to its lay application. Once again: Why this passion for watches? Maybe…maybe a premonition? Was he closer to death whenever he heard that ticking? As a combat officer in Vietnamese rice fields, was the ticking a warning of a forthcoming, oncoming death?" He whispered: "Am I a gash in somebody's biography, like loose skin on the surface of history?"

Franz Kafka writes: "You have grasped the kernel of the matter…"

"Which one would you want?" He asked himself, was I a palimpsest? All were silent ones, Mechanized.

Delacroix writes: "It is the intoxication of egoism."

He rejected the rectangular table, yet, he was convinced that watches were ticking away, just for him. When all of them ticked together, He was sure that chorus was an ultimate warning. Moving dials ticked away his life. Were all black dials funerals manufactured to tell him something? Black dials, which he preferred, reminded him of a priest's black robe. He wondered, smiling, were all black dials signaling his early death, or only the future (whenever that might happen, or, an everyday image of it.)

An old site bubbled up:

Jacques Brel singing:" Rappelle-toi, Barbara…"

But then, he praised his grandfather who had willed him a Patek

Phillipe. (From generation to

Generation

You do not keep one…) I wore mine for 11 years and then, when it came time for me to die,

Write my will, I willed it to my grandson. I knew that, one day, he, too, would will it to his son. (Had the colonel only waited to see the Project Z6 Black edition alarm movement-72 hours power reserve ZalumTM, exclusive Alloy, Harry Winston ad…)

(What he did not wish to tell anyone about his taste in watches, was because he dearly loved a black one… then he stopped, and listened to an internal ringing. He knew, in his heart of hearts (as the cliché goes) that Big Bang was a Brit. Death toll for thee!!…)

(Colonel Ames' new love affair came when he saw the black dial of the Cookoo watch, with its 3'4 and no screen and the G Shock GB 6900, with its beep or vibration. Colonel Ames was as polite as he could be, when sergeant Blake brought him back a Cookoo from the Schwartzwald.

He would have liked to exclaim: "Keep that fuckin' Cookoo for yourself!"

(In fact, he had a very negative feeling about his sergeant bringing him back, from a week-end leave, a Cookoo clock from the Black Forest. (If he were truthful enough, he might have said: "Keep that away from me!"

He strongly believed that us humans were prisoners of fear. No kidding!)

(Background singing from an old Al Jolson movie.)

He had caught site of a magnificent Girard-Perrigault, with its tourbillon, with three gold

Bridges. "Wow," he mumbled to himself, at that moment, that highly con-centrated birth moment in his memory.

If the kids interrupted, he'd send them back upstairs, to their bedroom, to finish their homework. His wife

Knew all about his discipline. However, if one thought they might be de-veloping into fine readers, there

Weren't any books around. Not a single book on top of the flat screen TV set.

Two weeks later, Clementine was in bed with a beaut. from Alaska. They soaped each other

In the shower. Unexpectedly, her former school lover bumped into her in an East Village Sake Joint. Perhaps,

For reasons that must have come from her Alaskan experience, she knew that National Security, nicknamed

Fort, had been hidden away inside Fort Meade, Md.

Everyone knew CIA

was located in

Camp Peary, VA.

Lt. Generals had the privilege of reading white ink.

Descriptions of intelligence operations in Afghanistan, and that included references to N.S.A. Who would ever have suspected the concealed return of Junior to D. C? In order to clarify what he had found, in the Hope that Families would collect their "Cherished" ones. Poplin had flown from

Yaroslav to Dulles, with a stop-over in London. Poplin carried a tiny cell

Phone.

He settled in his seat, and began reading his Tolstoy kindle "War and Peace."

Snoozed.

All Tolstoy's

Fault.

I knew nobody would ever wonder how his memory got unplugged, rereading whatever he could

Spit out, without calculation and, for example, see his Indian peace pipe hidden in his multi-pocketed

Jacket.

Junior remembered his grandfather's words: "You come from

Happy-Tribe. Never Forget It."

On his wall, he proudly exhibited a bi-lobbed basket, circa 1200 found in

Mogui Canyon, Utah. The entrance

To his apartment had a line of Nuxalb Masks. He didn't want to contradict
his Grandfather, but

He was sure he came

from the Mesquakie
region. How else could he have explained the so
rapid-cure of

His pregnant sister, when she went into an unin-
tended labor?

Beards fell asleep, or was that the way they wanted
it to

Appear?

Much closer to our own time, a Buffalo Hunt,
water colors on paper, sold in Taos, not far from

Agnes Martin's studio.

So many arms raised. Lots of horses and so many
buffalos, hunted down for their skins.

You could hear traditional songs in town, whooping it up for visiting tourists, but that
afternoon,

It rained, and gullies dribbled down the path between houses. Sitting on
rocking chairs, Indians looked at us

And smiled. A red
MG

Nearly drowned.

I asked myself how in the hell could I remember that scene? I

Suspect my memory, at times, renditioned to the present, without any warning. Then Agatha said: "Did you hear

that Sound of Silence?" She had that phenomenal ability of hearing it, but, when she could not, she would say:

"If only you could augment the Sound of Silence, then I'd be absolutely sure to hear it! (Somebody coughed.) I hear Silence everywhere, but there's no one there!!" For others, if only the train could

Jolt forward.

Agatha, whose nose was acute, smelled the dead in the last car. The new conductor, during This Q and A, said: "You'd never find this type of writing in the New

Yorker!"

The Stinking Smell of Death

And, to boot, like the train, Junior narrated his experiences to those

Middle-Aged Women, those Long

Island ladies, in their mid-sixties, all of whom, having lost their husbands, most probably to Prostate cancer, lived on their retirement funds and social security.

Cancer.

One of them, whose back ached, walked up and down the aisle, rubbing her back with both

Hands. She asked herself: "Why hadn't I asked for an aisle seat???" The toilet door said, in Capital

Letters:

"PLEASE COME IN"

And, in minuscule letters, "Please wash your hands if you work in the

Orient Express kitchen."

You know what you shouldn't do… Nothing seemed to curb the ladies'

curiosity. "Do

You have top clearance?"

Did she expect me to answer? He mumbled to himself, "In Good Time…" 19A asked where he was going next? I didn't want to reveal my Top Secret clearance and so, I smiled, as they do

In war-time movies to hide some Terrifying Truth.

121

THE SONG OF THE RENTAL AGENT AS AN ASIDE

A newly upholstered lady, riding on a wooden horse, seething, seeing her dead brother
On a 50 cent carnival horse...

So long ago, she asked

                    "in a writhing tone of voice."

"How much is it to rent a cloud?"

                    "Two Millions,

528, OOO DOLLARS and 32 cents."

(The book says it in clear print.)

 "Some of my best friends, from our Park Avenue Bridge Club, You may have recognized
them:

All Hollywood stars!!! (We play bridge every other Friday...)"

                    The Real Estate Agent tried to evacuate that info.

"I say to you, under my Friday night Chinese food breath, make up your mind,

You exploiting capitalists."

"My friends bought a whole floor

At the Marx."

(or was it at One Central Park West for lots more?)

Each flat for One million, 528, OOO, and 32 cents.

 All had TV built in their ceilings.

All loved James Bond's

Dr. No

From Russia with Love

Goldfinger

       When they stopped gabbing ((After their second martini)

They listened to 50 cent, Cool Diddy.

      Some preferred Ornette Coleman.

Made their money investing in private equity…

THE END OF THE REAL ESTATE SONG

Was it true US Government docs had

Used Indians in Guatamala to test some tough stuff to…but he

Had forgotten the rest.

In a few hours, he'd be interrogated, hand-cuffed, face a glass wall, and a computer

Placed gently on his lap.

"If, at any moment, you're uncomfortable, push U. Now, to our first question:

"Are you now or have you ever been a Trotskyite?" In dismay, I answered: "Who's Trotsky?" I didn't

Want to answer, but I did see the movie, and I knew Richard Burton had axed him to death. Where, at

That moment

was Frieda Khalo?

In college, I had taken a course on

Surrealism, so I knew André Breton

Was in Mexico City, at that very moment and, with Trotsky, wrote up (with André Breton) a "Manifesto for an

Independent Revolutionary art."

Not bad for such a contradictory statement in the shape of a Manifesto, quickly translated and printed in The Partisan Review.

 Now a steel rod hit his spinal cord.

He pushed "U."

Similar questions followed. He dreamt of reaching Brasov. No need for a nurse. A slight

(Strindberg writes: "What do you mean…")

Bleeding. A band-aid might do!

Then Another Question: "What do you think of our Techniques?" At that

Moment, Colonel Ames walked in. He was still mulling over his wife's possible misbe-havior. Would she have cheated on him? (All this in a viola phrasing.) And, if she did, with whom?

Would she wear nothing after the tango? Would she ask him to do the same or, as a Gentleman and a Decorated Officer, would he refuse to knead her?

I imagined hearing her working up a steam. "Ok." She would follow

Up with an "Ok."

"You're a gentleman and a West Point Graduate, so I can understand your hesitation. Here's my

Suggestion: I'll cover my eyes while you unzip. I'll take it from there!"

Or, would she be putting

The kids to bed, having double-checked their homework assignments? Still, she could have climbed the

Stairs and joined him.

Pillows, well positioned, sheets thrown on the floor. You could see, by Colonel Ames's face, he wasn't concentrating on the Interrogation. And if that wasn't enough,

He remembered trying to find an apartment in the XIV Arrondissement, not far from the Lion de Belfort, that awesome Lion, sitting there, blocking traffic or at least slowing it Down? "Hello! You really look so sad! Is there anything I can do?" ("Screw you!") Colonel Ames smiled.

One day, he might put all of those musings in a ms and perhaps a publisher might bite!! He could

Hear the Orient Express inching forward. A strangely dressed Official entered the compartment, saluted,

Took out a portable bilingual dictionary, flipped through it and then stopped at what he thought would be the...

(Interlude IV

(September 13, 2002) Apt. 12H

4:30 AM

Fourier makes a home call: 666 6666.

(IT MIGHT AS WELL BE TICKTICKTICKLIKELIKELIKE)

"A Carmel taxi is on its way."

"525 West End Avenue, corner 85th street."

Be there at 7:30. Promptly."

A repetition:

"Please, send a black limo."

"We'll be there, at 525 West End Avenue."

                    "Where's youze goin?"

"To my cemetery!"

A friend sat in the back.

                    A Little Song on the Intercom:

            "O Where O where has my little Poplin gone?"

"Fourier, dear friend, why go back? Go forward to the next station. Take hold of yourself."

"Fill' er up."

Fourier thinks, thinks of love in a communal setting, thinks with difficulty, forgetting time. He knows too much.

Mrs. Friedman,

His first grade teach at PS 54, said something like:

"Louder, please. Remember what you said before."

Appropriate entry. "Zoon U vil got do do …"

He knew English wasn't his native language. He blamed his

3rd grade teacher for doing more singing in class than perfecting his rudimentary English. He hoped someone might speak Serbo-Croatian.

Blank stares. Poplin's scared.

If anyone of those jerks

Suspected I was here, what would they do to the Others? He wouldn't say a word. In any case, he was

Sworn to secrecy. The fact that a large number… but then, who could count on who had been maimed or

Killed? Agatha stared out through the clotted window. "Let's stay as calm as possible!"

A few drops of rain.

Cries in the Background.

("When you reach the border, wait until midnight. A professional will take you to your next

Destination. Keep low.

Do not smoke your pestilential Hungarian smokes. When you spot the

train, with its new engine, recently placed in its place, approach it with Prudence. They may still be roaming

Terrorists

Hiding and then, who knows! We may have droned them all to death!")

To conceal their Terror

Agatha mumbled Lon Chaney's 1923 THE HUNCHBACK OF NOTRE

DAME.

"Had anyone ever read Victor Hugo's classic?"

(Solange raised her hand, the way she had always done in class.)

Agatha interrupts: "Don't you

Prefer Charles Laughton's version?"

And, she added,

"How great Tom Hulce's voice when the three

Gargoyles spoke."

Anything to pass the time of day and night. I think I know, if you think cocaine, you'll THINK COCAINE, and you'll go straight to Sherlock Holmes!"

Then, someone called our attention to Colonel Ames and his- by- now

Dusty soldiers, ready to revenge the brutal murders of some of our best:

wrists tied, ankles pierced with

Thin wooden sticks,

gathered near a huge oak tree, in what remained of the High Grass. As their Collective Signature defined their acceptance of the document, they poured gasoline on their bodies and scorched

Them to Death.

Nothing remained. All we could find were bones and what was left of their boots.

Hideous reminder that our local narco-trafficker war lords, hiding in nearby mountains, probably in inter-

Connected caves, concealing a terrorist network, were the only ones able to work with a well-trained donkeys

Able to get us there, especially helped by our overly-paid local warriors! I do not remember anyone

Greeting us with such details. Makes your stomach turn around. To get my mind over such matters,

Charles Bernstein writes:" Maybe that event was to be the subject of a sequel…"

I heard one of the Lindenhurst ladies say: "Why are we all sobbing?" I

said: "Just to stop answering

Their questions."

"Had she seen a red 1986 Jag., sitting there, in their parking lot?" She

Answered that her mother, now in a fenced-in Florida community for elderly people, with men on

One side

Women on the other.

She asked if anyone had ever dubbed you "Poplin?"

"In Rome," I

Replied.

"Had he ever seen middle-aged American females from Eastern Long

Island?"

"No." She gulped

Down her Pellegrino from her plastic bottle.

You could see she was escaping from her Recent Past

As an Executive gold American Express first class traveler, a trip for which she
had laid out 12 thousand US dollars and that, just to walk

Around Rome.

With her musings (she whispered to herself) "What's with an X-max tree on

Her neighbor's lawn with flashing lights?" She murmured to herself, it was really

"Now or Never! Either I get one, too, or I'll torch hers."

After all, Lindenhurst is a relatively small Jewish community where everybody

Knows Everybody,
Except, of course, those illegal Mexes we hire to mow our lawns! My

Other friends,

Living in one house next to another,

Either would do what I was planning to do or Else… come up with

Another suggestion. In any case, something we neighbors could not do. I

Was the only one with a pound of Free Will.

On Saturdays, I didn't pray,

Pray, like our husbands used to do, kippas on their heads, and holding an
elegantly sewn Turkish bag, holding

Our prayers.

At that moment of Calm, they had to come up with something else, given
the fact—

Especially visible in all our mental mirrors that, there we were, middle aged
ladies, wearing tight tights

(One of us, and, I've forgotten who it was, said what we were wearing was
indecent, something like

Those female

"agents provocatrices"

In a Roman male spermy dream magazine.

(John R. Searle writes: "The thing which is a rose is red.")

Forlorn lips sketched out of a rapid purchase in a local Rome store. (I've forgotten the name of the square.) "Ah! For our friends left

Behind!!"

If only they had been told about that Roman Kosher restaurant!! She remembered how she

Had walked into her new kitchen, with a new Self-Defrosting Fridge and a new Marble Counter, all .

Done by illegal Mexes.

(Long live our illegal Mexican peasants on murals, painted on the wall of the New

School.)

And yet, when she closed the door of the fridge, she heard a squeak. It hadn't been oiled right.

"Must call him back! That cheating Mex."

She asked her friends if their fridge had a squeak…

Been redone by those same Mexes?

By the way, had they located new addresses for Kosher restaurants in

Rome?

"Anything but Jewish Pasta!"

I'll never be able to look at myself in my bathroom mirror if I step on my scale!!" Were

There any streets in Rome with no cars?

She had an aversion for Foreign-Made Cars, even when she sat

Quietly on her front porch, rocking, like a Florida retiree, living on her husband's pension.

There was rarely a car or a truck passing by. "At my

Age, noises hurt my ears.

I really can't think, with all that traffic." She smiled: "I can hear drones," she muttered. "If any swooshed down my street, I'd phone."

According to the town's

Rules in Lindenhurst, It was forbidden to honk your horn. As she thought of those de-
pressing possibilities, she hummed a song from "South Pacific," one of her favorites, sung
by Mario Lanza. I was

Sure he was a Roman!! A soldier, who had nothing to lose, said: "Couldn't you wipe that
fuckin' grin off your

Face?"

As she thought back, for a moment, when she thought (could she?) she heard cries from
next door or, she wondered, out loud,

What her neighbors were doing? Maybe they had overheard my thoughts? And was she
as ready as was to set

Fire to all X-Mas trees in the neighborhood, since Jews do not fete Christmas!

Hattie died four days later.

The lights hadn't yet been taken down from those trees. We hired a black limousine (it may have been the last one around) and followed the hearse to our

Favorite Cemetery, as it was our custom.

Later, we brought a red Long Island wine from the North Shore.

and a Vermont Camembert. We all sat down. Some of us on her new

White leather couch, others on her white bridge chairs, taken out of the closet, near the entrance, near the coat rack closet.

All of us knew she was a Special Person, but nobody knew how to pull it off.

At that moment, words tended to disappear when you wanted to recall

them, like children hiding in the far end of a school playground in the yard.

But we knew one fact: We knew she simply adored Ryman, and she went even

Further.

She had had all her ceilings painted white, wiping out the red, previously painted above her head. She had, a while back, asked some unemployed painter to paint all of her furniture white, including the piano. Nobody knew where she had ever gotten that idea into her head!

Nobody could make out why she was always smiling.

She did mention, en passant, that the smog was so thick in Cairo, she had to wash her hair twice a Day.

She insisted that the reddish sandy smog was so vomitive, she could only dream of seeing a perfect white

Ceiling, glistening above her.

She said that, in a very affirmative voice!

Then they sliced ten apples and poured honey in a small dish and each one of us dipped our apple slice into the honey.

"Anybody for Lipton or a

Manhattan?"

With her eyes half- closed, she thought she could remember a dark-hair young man who had picked her up, near the cemetery entrance, a year after her husband's death, when she walked around and placed little stones on his

Grave.

What a fascinating place, like Père Lachaise where cats slept on graves.

A black-haired young man, standing straight as an arrow in a Western
outfit, without a stitch of hair on his chest. He had

picked her up at the entrance to the cemetery. She thought he was

Gorgeous. She managed to have him

Come to her home as a Visiting Scholar.

(She couldn't remember what country he came from or why he was in the
US. But those were accidental questions. She quickly shoved them aside.
She said to herself: "What purpose would that have served?")

In the morning, I would bring him tea and Islamic

Flat bread purchased on Atlantic Avenue. There she was, naked in her
bedroom, with her ceiling painted white. She held a wipe in her left hand.

She said: "Come closer to my side." (Pointed to her

Black heels, under the bed.)

She said: "Are you ready for a little Lindenhurst surprise?" She wiped his ass

Repeatedly. "Listen to the following quote and you might echo it or…not!"

Jean-Jacques Rousseau: "Ainsi s'éclipsèrent en un instant toutes mes grandes espérances."

"If you make the slightest noise, you'll regret it."

She poured hot wax in his ass. You could hear him

Scream: "I never suspected such a thing might happen, here, in Eastern

Long Island. And especially at 72 Clover."

I shouted in agony. Tried, without any hope, to turn around. The pain

was unbearable.

She smiled all

The time, hummed a tune from "South Pacific." He said: "Get rid of that stupid smile."

She pinched his

Cock with her right hand. She whispered:

"Huba, Huba, Huba—don't need that rubba!"

He shot an abundance of sperm into her willing mouth.

She tied his wrists to the bed post.

"Now, I'd like to show you my show. It's part of my old Doctoral Research, all of that, as I'm

Preparing you to die."

She sets up her digital camera and focused on his body. "Then, I'll stuff your

Mouth with cotton candy.

By the time mommy rings the doorbell, as she usually does at this time of the

Afternoon. She does that, not to disturb my studies. By the time I let her in, I had already dug a grave in the cellar for

YOU

As I had done for so many others!"

She coughed with pleasure. Then, I'd help her climb the stairs to her second floor bedroom. Every night, mother washed her false teeth with her new electric tooth

Brush.

My birthday gift.

Sometimes, she wondered why her daughter
hadn't found a man she could marry, even a

Guy with two kids.

Sometimes, she thought she heard a man's voice, but that happened for such a Brief Moment! She had, probably, invented all those voices, or so I thought. In the bathroom, staring at her face in the mirror, she

Thought she might get a series of injections to get rid of her aging spots, and especially those lines around her mouth,

When she laughed. When she thought about a possible match for her daughter.

She remembered her husband, dead now for the past five years (was that true??)

After retirement, he had picked up the bass fiddle.

Not bad at all!!

She went to the cemetery, twice a year. When she went with her bouquet, she was always accompanied by two weeping widows doing the same.

TITLE :

                              RATS

scurrying rats

Death nibbled

A corps in darkness, a corps, Had
it been a year? A lost identity

Still

Sounds remained

What's left of them, but in a recording of
a lullaby? After death, Grass was reli-
giously mowed by unemployed Mexes.
Dissembled,

exiled. Next spring

A replay

Flowers, black veils

A mul-
tiplication of tiny stones

Solitary rain drops

(A friend, to make him happy,
had slipped Nudes in his coffin,
for entertainment. Images shot
by Drtikol.)

"My life has been a
poem." Thoreau

'A long is
this long ago."   '
Cymbeline

They prepared their
luggage for a move
to Tampa. One thing
I do remember!! My
daughter

Is an avid camper, I knew that,
because she bought a new duf-
fel bag every month. One day, I

couldn't

Find Daddy's bass fiddle case. I guess I'm going batty!
At my age, you can't even trust a family memory! One
night, I thought I heard daughter having what

Seemed to me to be a nightmare. In fact, she was having a tiny night-
mare where she found herself at

Court, asked if she were responsible for some Hideous
Crime. "Is it true you've been down to the

Cellar where your father grew mushrooms?

("Every Sunday, he'd pile them into a three egg omelet,
as they do in France.)

"Do you have

Anything else to say…"

"The Jury knows very well what it means to forget
where one's Father's bass fiddle case hides.

"It could've disappeared, so many things remain on the
periphery of The Mind!

Yes. Let me quote

Pier Paolo Pasolini: "It's better to be the Enemy of the people than an

Enemy of reality." ("Unhappy Youths.")

In such a fake-dream-like mind-set, only a single question remained. "Has the jury reached a verdict?"

"We have, your honor,"

As they handed the judge an envelope, with the result of their deliberations.

"Will the accused please stand up. "How do you find…"

And,

As quickly as a summer downpour dries up, they said, in perfect harmony: "The jury finds you

"Guilty."

She thanked the jury and

Loudly proclaimed: "Long Live American Justice!" The public applauded

Vehemently! "Now, in these times

Of political turmoil, what a Great Breath
of Fresh Air!" I had already checked out
your weight and Height. "All will soon be
over!

Notin's too good for my Clients! "Please,
slip the duffel bag over your

Head and slide it down your body.

You'll be next to Fritsy." Then a knock

at the front door. Three

Stooges, one dumber than the other, stood
there. "Is this 72 Clover

Street? We've got a coffin to

Deliver." "Christ!" She says to herself: "Not another
one!!" One of the three Stooges, hearing cries for

Help, called the Lindenhurst police

on his cell. When duty calls, driv-
ers lend their ears. Then, the three jumped into their
hearse and drove away. They hadn't even left a Calling
Card!

Half a step down Clover, not far from the public
library,

You could see a red Jag crushed against a
tree.

"Come with shovels," The stooge told the
police. "In any

Case, we're bound to make the headlines! Like the
Marx Brothers!" The Police dredged the river.

She hadn't been seen for a

Week.

A helpful stooge yelled out: "I found her social Secu-
rity: 854

349 2789! And only parts of her

Body... Looks like she jumped in, like

Ophilia, before settling down in a whore-
house!

A Gentler breath and lots of tiny pebbles
below the surface swimming like fish.

"What a terrible way to die! I mean, limb
by limb, as if her head had been gulped
down by a hungry shark!"

By the time he reached Dulles, Poplin had
forgotten he had ever read anything in the

local paper. At the

Airport, by the time he had walked
down the gang plank, a blue- black limo
whisked him away. Hadn't he

Been told he had been rebaptized? His
New Name was Poplin. In an office, ques-
tions bombarded him.

An officer had his feet on the desk,
smoked a Cuban cigar. "Now, I'll show
you what happened when

One of our crusaders, facing Death, as
should a good Catholic…" He stopped.
He'd forgotten the 7th Crusade.

"We've done it! He passed all the tests!
Now, he's really, really, ready for his new
assignment!" A

Couple of shots, or were there more in his glass?

A single malt whiskey from Islay, and he would be-
come an

Excellent Informant! But

Then, on his own, he began talking. "I did see

them killed. I barely heard our Drones.

(Practical silence.)

Everywhere!"

Women, in the first limousine, had been
forced to step out and hide in the High
Grass. I heard the

Sound of machine guns. In the distance, I saw three
farm houses, one on fire. Our

Drones had done their job.

Tanks surrounded the three women. Poplin imagined
he was being

Questioned.

"Poplin, I've got sad news for me and you!
After all your successful field familiarity in
and around Kandahar AND, TO ADD TO
THAT, YOUR

REPORTS ON

TORTURE...

Defense wants you! You'll be promoted to
colonel with a nice raise! Sorry to see you
go...Good luck on your next assignment."

He may still have been a se-
cret CIA agent, there to write up a Report.
Was he on a Secret Mission? He couldn't
remember. Somebody asked him if he
was sure about who he was and what he
thought he had to accomplish.

Looking back to a recent past, he made
believe he had been brain-washed or his
memory, side-tracked, had blanked out.

Somebody had taken over his mind and
made him a Servant of The Cause, or per-
haps a Killer or, at least, someone upon
whom others thought they might count
on. Something like in a movie. Was every-
thing he had seen and heard a mirage? His
invented memory? He could barely make
out what the lady was asking,

Sitting next to him. He didn't want to explain why he
was reading

Simone de Beauvoir:

"Pendant la liquidation de la Révolution la femme
jouit d'une liberté anarchique. «

I said, reluctantly, "My seat had been se-
lected by the office," and they said: "Pack

your duffel bag. You'll be driven to the
airport."

The elderly lady, sitting next to him, took
out a little white vomit bag. "You don't
mind? I

Can't sit too long, my stomach gets whispy. I can't tell
you how many times this has happened to me! My
mind no longer belongs to me!

Next trip, I promised myself, I'll bring my
own brown bag!"

Then she vomited what the stewardess
had served her a minute ago. She had
opted for chicken.

Four floors below Arlington Cemetery, the

CIA had trained

Him to hear from a distance. This time, as the

vomit crept up her throat, he heard it.

"You?"

"Do you know what's going to happen
to...

You might take a
guess, much like in a writers' group.

It's all in the lines."

Now, that he understood, he could ask himself: "is Writing a Word or is it a word? is it a Mirage of a Word? Or is it a weird repetition? Or would it all be in the

Movement of the hand?

He thought, for a minute, and then continued asking himself: "was it all in the mind?

Were I a metaphysician, I might be able to deal with such a Problem!

What's your thoughts

On this matter? It's as simple as that!! "

(Intolerable recurrence…)

He said: " Read Aristotle's

PROSE/POETRY AS A

TACTILE SUBSTANCE

My own thoughts: Am I an identity? or could you take me for another?

BULL SHIT

"I heard machine gun fire from below.

How could I, even momentarily, forget my
orders to penetrate Kandahar by night?

To make the writing easier, was it part of
redefining the space between words, as
they become loosely interconnected?

Would Words have taken over the text?

Was all of that a mirage? Did I really believe, sitting
next to the smell of vomit, that all of that miss-hearing
could have been anchored in an auditory mirage? All I
could hear

Was the a

Absence of SOUND FOLLOWED BY mat-
ters of facts...

(Were I a beginner, I could have been an
envelope-world.

(Was it like the BOOK of THE DEAD?)

"Did I

Really believe all the above? Kandahar held up by a
paper clip? I

saw a Drone fire on one of the farm

Houses below.

The smell of perfumed flesh.

In any case, as you well know, I'm sworn to secrecy.
Were I to inform the Fat Lady squatting next to me, I
was afraid I'd be assigned to the

38th parallel with other
southern draftees from … I could see my
boots

dribbling down a drizzly path. A lieutenant told me I
should wear

Basketball sneakers when the rains came.

I heard Agatha singing an old English
song.

I heard Agatha listening to distant voices in a foreign
tongue.

Eggs. Butter. Muffins.

As if they were fleeing from a burning
House. Out of all those Particles of Mean-
ing, I could see Colonel Ames, sitting at
his desk, working on a

Novel he hoped to turn into a Novel, with
a new-born narrative, Identifiable charac-
ters, and a couple of

Reminders of the past. Then he thought of
a proper beginning. "There they were, two

Cops in sun-bleached blue uniforms, climbing up a
wooden staircase. At the head of the stairs, two

Gorgeous High School Juniors…" That
was enough.

(Scratch out the preceding.)

Ask them for their beach pass.

They asked where the hell were the Mexes

Who worked here?

They answered, in harmony: "he's wash-
ing up a foot pool of diarrhea in the men's Toilet."

When he got out, holding a filthy mop
above his smelly feet, they asked him to
wash up in the

Foot shower. Which he did.

Then they took him to a waiting van and opened the
back door. Pushed him inside. Five other Mexes were
on the floor, ankles tied with electric wires on their
knees. They

Both went back up the stairs.

"Take one of the Juniors and take her back
to the Van.

Undress her."

She wore a simple High school blue bathing suit.

Six Mexes. fucked her with a couple of Spanish words
thrown in.

As they

Breathed, she violently twisted around. (Much had
already been done in Egypt and India where violent
sexual attacks on young women had become a qua-
druple daily anal act.)

The van drove down Sea Spray Road.
Invalids

Looked on, sitting there, on the deck. Mary heard a
mother yelling: "Freddy, get here this very minute or
you'll never get ..(Seriously, he said to himself, would
repetition reach back to

"memory ?")

They saw (as always, and they suspected it, every time
they spoke, that they had spoken the same language as
before.

A tricky strategy.)

Seagulls landed, flapped their wings.

Old invalids, sitting on invalid chairs,
saw a couple walking over a horse shoe crab. Kids
picked up sea shells. Families crouching under colorful
beach umbrellas. Babies sleeping.

Later, they said, in quasi-unity, "how
disgusting to see those Trash Cans over-
flowing!"

Old women lived together after their husbands' disap-
pearance.

They found pleasure in reasserting their views. If any-
thing had been momentarily forgotten, each one could
come up with an invented sequence, even if no con-
nections existed.

Satisfaction.

Had they only known the van and its
acts…?

(Colonel Ames re-read his newly-minted text, but
then, decided to add a few more words. Spacing, he be-
lieved, was an essential part of writing, to make a point
out of nothingness.

"Good enough to shake up

memory?"

They drove down to the intersection. Turned left at the
bank. Then down Main Street, turned

Right, passed the movie house, and made a sharp left
at the Police

Station. He added, taking into account

The latest debate:

Should illegal Mexes be forced into a ditch?

On our side, filled with

Alligators

On their side,

Sharks ready to chomp on

their legs?

Some even thought of a head in a boas'
Mouth!

According to a New York Times article, The Mex. Pres.
accused the US of dumping criminals on

His side of the border, ACCORDNG to US
strategies, 2000 miles long, right on our
Border, he insisted.

The van dropped off the Mexes. at the Police Station. Then they went to the local diner, close to the movie house.

"Make mine an apple pie with a scoop of

Vanilla."

"What about you?" asked the old lady, ready to go home.

"Same."

In walked the chief of Police.

"Got news for you boys! The Mexes tried to get away. We shot them,

then we found soft ground behind the station, and we buried them.

We saved you the trouble! We should'a opened the back door,

and let them fall out on a deserted road." It must have been before sunset and nobody had yet…

Was there, then, in a gravely voice, a resonance of an irreducible conviction, hiding beyond a banality (see above) hiding beyond banalities, even the voice was hesitant in acknowledging itself as a fictitious memory: an irresistible imperative? A vehemence?

Jacques Lacan writes: "Is what thinks in
my place, then, another I?" Could it have
been a "somebody" stealing his memory?"

Kids were piled up in mini-vans, with col-
orful beach umbrellas and folding chairs,

in the back of their Dodge 4x4. Two cops

checked

out old magazines, like the Saturday
Evening Post or, on the shelves, old beer
mugs.

After having

Gobbled up their pies à la mode, they wondered if
those Mexes. had used

BB guns to shoot squirrels off…

(Colonel Ames mumbled to himself as if, at this inter-
stice, an applicable quote might fit here.)

Peggy Kamuf writes:" We recall that Abe-
lard represents…")

the road to Riverhead.

Colonel Ames reread what he had written
down. Smiled. He said to himself,

"That should do the trick for openers: A mix and match: squirrels, Without ever remembering my so-called dumb memory working overtime, I

Heard the stewardess ask if I wanted Chicken or Beef? Others had asked, in advance, a Veggie,

A Kosher one.

Later, I hoped to go to the beach with my Beach pass glued on my rear window

...

(What a movie that could make!)
I thought Ames might be
someone's invention, somebody
who had invented him. What
about myself as Poplin? I saw
skins sun-tanned, bathing suits,
tight as tight and
I saw kids waiting on line

For their ice-cream.

Parents waiting for burgers and fries, and, when they came, drowning them in ketchup

On both, and drinking diet cokes, as if they hadn't ever had a drink in this swanky beach club…

On the wooden platform, looking

Out to sea,

Invalids had been rolled up, staring at the Red and

Black Flags hoisted over the Life Guard Stand, checking out babies, with their overweight parents, dipping them in wavelets. He could

Imagine Col. Ames signing a letter to a New York publisher and signing his letter with a cliché: "Yours,

Sincerely."

A month later, he received an encouraging reply signed:

"My Best."

And he, then- the publisher- added, "I

Hope to see you on the 38th floor! You'll have a Great View of Lower Manhattan." Ames

Suddenly remembered he hadn't

mentioned his wife, a nurse in a

Manila hospital where he had been

Sent to recuperate from a leg injury,

When she heard others speak. She knew they had taken
another train of

thought. Still, she was proud of having
learned, by heart, large chunks of Freud's Introduction to his Special-
ty. However, she could not circumscribe what she had been taught
at an early age. She asked herself, when we pray, do we not follow
Abraham's laws, or at least those laws dictating what we are allowed
to eat, how we should kill an animal, when to eat and when not to.
She knew, and Freud must have known that, when he wrote about:
The Giver of Laws. I call him the Unconscious of Origins. Wasn't it a
penchant, I mean, reading facts another way? One wasn't that

Distance a way from another? One day, psychoanalysts
would consider such delectable prohibitions as proof of
difference, difference we called, without ourselves, ac-
knowledging similarities. Why then did Charles Martel
"save" the West from its partner Civilization? A rejec-
tion, via war, characterized a disassembled reality. A
child's game. Freud understood all of that. He went back
to the Greeks for a metaphor. He spoke in a convingly
voice: "Next year in Athens." And he whispered, once a
year, a pilgrimage to the

Rock of Oedipus.

Sometimes, I stared at myself in an invisible mirror,
checking out my clothing, hearing my muted prayers,
eating prohibited food in a chinese restaurant. Others,
in the "A," group, mumbled something. It could have
been that night's menu. The men I knew wore a dif-
ference on Fridays, at funerals, at marriages, at a boy's
blood, being sucked out by an official of their religion.
How close to Freud's meta-thoughts!

For our ceremonial meal, we had a yearly family
Thanksgiving dinner. I wasn't an acceptable cutter-
of-meat, but, I did cut up the turkey with a serrated
electric knife. My family

Applauded and said, if one day, I

should meet the enemy, I could cut him in half!

She said she adored Fritz

Lang because of his dark shadows darkness.

Anyhow, I told them I had nightmares

when I saw myself slicing up a human being

with that electric knife! (Was I, perhaps,

conforming to a Greek tragedy?) Nobody believed me.
My "technician of the head" told me that was only a dream, prob-
ably aimed at my father.

I told her we had a musician in the family. My Father
played the bass

fiddle. He bought the most elegant case and had his
initials sown on it. Was that his way of assuring his
particularity or perhaps some way back

to a souvenir repressed?

My 3F brothers laughed in unison.

They asked

What then was authenticity in language?

A triple manifestation of language?

Skimming in

Unison, I added I could see blood on the table, next to the mashed
potatoes.

My new wife thought that wasn't funny at all.

"White or Dark?"

IMMOBility

TICKTICKTICK LIKELIKELIKE

(You like student talk in multiplicity.)

If only you could pretend imagining what was going through Col.
Ames'

mind, you'd be able to read

The following:

"As far as I'm concerned, it's 6:30 in the morning. He knew, with great precision, that one man's time never corresponded to another's. One heard voices, the other a ticking sound, a repetitive, and perhaps a menacing ticking. The colonel heard that sound and, early on, made up his imagination. Sounds had become language with syllables and consonants ticking away, falling into place. What was left to be done? A translation. But where were the bilingual dictionaries or, to be more precise, Freud

apart (if that were conceivable, as if I could recall it!…) a bilingual adept like the one sitting in front of me. I had not the slightest doubt that his learning contained the translation of a spoken dream. I might have been overly optimistic, but I had no other options. He seemed to me to note down my words to be, later on, in the privacy of his office, as he remembered those pages in Freud dealing with translation- and they were numerous. He put them together, as he had done with my recitations, as if I had memorized my dreams in a play and, with ease, pour out, in a memorized (so called…) manner, what, I didn't know, lurked within me. At night, after getting up, I shook his hand, made another appointment. I heard my voice, and I could barely agree with what was being said. Was truth a narration, an inconsequential series connected to a possible

reality ? Or, if I were able to voice introspection, I'd run into Freud's idea of displacement, as if my disappeared memory had been transferred elsewhere or transformed into an alarm clock- dream. Was I aroused, only if I could say or stage a palimpsest—something hidden below I'd never allow to enter my thoughts, too anxious ridden.

 Could it be,

Perhaps, a moment of free willed association? If he talked about forgotten dreams, could I then enter the imaginary Black Box with his suggestions? I thought I had it all figured out. He told me it might be a distortion, a sign of a voicelessness, a forgotten attic memory? Or could I consider my anxiety, and then, could I tell him, if I whispered that, somehow, I was responsible for the momentary disappearance of my owned memory? Anxiety's repression? Or again, taking into "account," displacement, evoke (give voice to…) what I thought might have been a sign relegated to absence? Would my listener suggest to himself that, what I was saying, freely in front of his notebook, might be a form of censorship, an entrance to a so-called past? Or would he think, to himself, according course work and his readings, a form of verbal regression, my unknown way of disguising a compromise?

I stared at him as he "took" me down.

Was I, for an instant, my verbal escape?

Would he, silently, at the tip of his blue ball point pen, say to himself, what I said was a sign of paralysis, an invisible piece of a conceded hand-language, in fact, or, as some might call it, a defective testimony? Or a part in a play I had forgotten?

In my memory, or was it so? (Sometimes I wondered if I could not recover my memory by fracking?) There, myself at my side, a Passover meal, matzo ball soup, bitter herbs, a hard-boiled egg, a finger dipped in a glass of wine. Prayers reminded me that, if we did indeed eat bitter herb, it corresponded to Egyptians who embittered the life of our ancestors. Then, at the head of the table, professor so and so insisted that there would never be a Palestinian State, but then, again, a graduate student of religion popped in with memorized words. "In the name of Allah, the compassionate, the merciful. 76: I. " Then he went on (much to the distaste of a number of friends around that rectangular table) "O children of Israel! Remember my (special) favor which I bestowed upon you, and that I preferred you to other (nations) for my Message." But then a warning Addressed to the Infidel: "Tearing out (his existence) right out of his skull." If they're hungry, let them eat crème brûlée. (His wife's speciality.) (He didn't want to quote his Humanities course work, and quote on… a quote: "…and the pagans shall burn forever in the fire of Hell." Then, for good luck, another quote, in French, from the Bible: "Il y avait une fois au pays d' Ours un homme du nom de Job…"

She was a religious pharmacist, preparing a trip to France, under one condition: in any town or city, there had to be a Kosher restaurant. "I'll never set foot in Avignon." She settled in Carpentras, not far from the re-dedicated synagogue. She never suspected that, behind the Palais des Papes, as of the 14th century, there was, and still is, the Avignon deli, serving sour pickles and cole slaw, together, with a now, lean pastrami, and the same for corned beef- all that cushioned in a Pain Poilane (no rye bread available.)

But the English Jewish pharmacist made sure, out of respect for the Jewish invasion of New York City, to rent a flat on Orchard

Street, above a fusion Japanese restaurant.

As for Hettie, before her death, she, too, made sure a Kosher restaurant had to be found in every southern French town. If she couldn't find one, she didn't care: her travel agent would already have lined up a splendid touristic guided tour, starting with Santa Maria in Aracoely and then the Temple of Jupiter! He did say: "don't miss San Marco Square in Venice! Take a picture, even if Venice is under water! Eat white pizza! If you need to extend your visits to Rome and Florence, buy Gallimard's guide book to those two cities and then he added, memorize the needed info. If you have any doubts as to your ability to memorize, memorize again, ask one of those tourist guides to give you eyes!!"

She knew that, for a good deal of money, her travel agent had it all figured out.

Her agent, knowing she had majored in English, asked her if she had memorized "The Song of Hiawatha." As far as I knew, something remained, back there in my mind, unless my memory hid in a bramble, and I had to select, all by myself, the needed stuffing! If I had difficulties, then, in an inner whisper, I'd ask for help from a divine erection (I did remember Michelangelo's "Christ on the cross," genitals visible, and then, that same painter had done it again for "The descent from the cross.")

Then again, he suspected that consonants and vowels, when they put themselves together, formed a link to an "elsewhere."

She heard flushing in the toilet.

She asked, to be different, if he knew the Pentateuch and the Haftorah?

He whispered to himself, what if, something like a link, could be summoned to the fore and his narration renew itself?

Waiting for them to land. We played with an equivalent situation, this time, as he had done it before, lying on his back, hearing words emerge, as did planes out of a dark cloud of the body.. They made murmuring noises, their own language. Would that have been my language, a language I ignored, something I didn't even know was totally "there," like a piece of myself as somebody else, and with the science of translation, Freud could have deciphered it. In fact, maybe nobody would ever know, buried in a poem or a piece of prose… or even better, in a dialogue exchanged on my mind's stage.

One was inaudible. Clouds may have disturbed its flow of Silence. Had the identifying propeller been shot down? (Maybe pieces had been scattered, like memory?) Shot down?

Had the motor failed? Run out of fuel? Others saw the pilot ejected from the cockpit, followed…

                    (By a parachute
opening up. Check out some war
movie.)

                    Whoosh
        whoosh

Crinkly fires in the distance. Gun fire closer
to the train. In fact, the only thing waiting on
the floor,

Behind everybody's sight, were tutus, and petals of wilted flowers at a
grave site, where they said a

Shark had been buried, left behind, as the rest of the Belarus Company,
dead after their rehearsal. At

That very moment, and again, at still another, at that very same moment, the

Conductor, with his fat fingers, popped in

With an undelivered letter for Claudine. She opened it, "Hope all's well
with you. Looking forward to

Seeing your pictures of those faraway lands! Yours, in the hope of see-
ing you soon."

Claudine turned to Agatha: "Why are you looking so glum?" Agatha
answered: "I was dreaming of Lon Chaney's 1923

HUNCHBACK OF NOTRE DAME.

I had just finished reading Victor Hugo's 1831 novel, as I might have told

You.

I've always been fascinated by intertextual translations as a her-
menuetical problematics. (Another memory problem?) (See John
D. Caputo.)

Meaning, what really happens when you slide from novel to film, from
one space to another. Here's another example: Charles Laughton's ver-
sion and…I especially love those gargoyles speaking through Tom Hulce's
voice! If I close

My eyes, even for a minute, I hope I can read my own 33 novels where I portrayed Hercules le Poirot (a Belgium

Elegant, nicely mustachiod) who spoke on radio and frequently ap-
peared in films, interpreted

Or...intertexually interpreted by John Offat, Albert Finney, Sir Peter

Ustinov, and plenty of others

Around the western world.

I wanted him to live in an Art Nouveau building, unlike Baker Street
Holmes

And Watson. And, if you're a "lumpen proletariat," maybe you might con-
sider the house maid who lets

People in through the otherwise locked front door and comes in with tea
at the very moment Holmes is shooting up cocaine in his arm.

Agatha also got a hint of the 1848 Revolution, having read Flaubert's

"Sentimental Education."

O!

Lord

Feet

Are my Delight

Your

YOU CHANGED THE WORLD

She remembered her travels out of college.

Sidelined memories harked back to adolescence… (Through
an invisible partition of the mind, others listened as I spoke.)

> Played with sub-machine guns with other kids in the neighborhood
> .Right here:
>
> Repeat:

> Derrida: "My interest is to leave a trace on the history of the French lan-
> guage…via my own memory…"
>
> > "Will you, please,
> >
> > Concentrate on a glass…
> >
> > Play My Game."

(Repeat the above as a virgin text.)

> Could all that be an Unwilling Sound rejected?
>
> Repeat…Mimed memory. Help me save my past:
>
> Cratylus
>
> Dionysius
> LEIBNITZ Rus-
> sell Thrax

Lena Horne

Zo mani mor

 Frank Sinatra: "Memory is a tramp."

Somehow, I was familiar with   "

"Your disturbed memory."

"By the way, no canned food, and no large bottles of sugar-filled soft drinks."

One, in particular, wore a Bergdorf Goodman's two piece grey suit with a blue sweater underneath.

Picabia says: "Ma tête se gonfle"   And
added:

« 'Zurich—"Mouvement Dada."

"Revue Dada"

"Galerie Dada"

(Did it ever cross your muted memory that something could have hung on a wall? What about:

Blashfied's: "The evolution of Civilization?")
(HOW MANY "repeats" are enough?)
TICKTICKTICKLIKELIKE

"Justine or the Misfortune of Virtue."

"like they used to do after a month in the country."

Repeat

Mother said: "Repeat."

Did she ever mean it when her glasses fell on the kitchen
               floor? "My memory's shot to death." (?)

She insisted she heard men's voices and rarely a ticking
               downstairs. She'd say: "O! Memory where hast Thou
               Gone?"

(Bette Davis and George Brent in: "STAR.")

And I whispered...

Rimbaud weeps: "Memory is anoth-
er's..." Repeat

Repeat

Repeat

Rimbaud smiles: "Get rid of Baudelaire. I hate his prose
poems." They approached me.

                    I yelled: "Colonel
                         Cryptov."

I want to go home again. (I didn't even smile, as they do in anthologies.) "Now," she said,
                    "the electric rods."

                    "A turn. Now."

        (Kama Soutra suggests: "Le jagdana ou milieu du corps.")

        "Show him three young naked women."

        (If you ask me, I wanna have dem, too!) Repeat

                    Repeat

183

(He whispers: "Isn't repetition a way of recuperating memory?) The Orient Express

(Do not be shy: Repeat…) Repeat

I'll start with Akhmatova's:

"air"

or a poem by Elizabeth Bishop:

stove,

And, floated like a swan

Through smoky, golden

"another minute, then indoors, besides,

keep on reading a book."

NURSE's DREAM

Sees herself as a tourist in Manhattan. Knows she's married to a colonel. (Never crossed her tourist mind to ask which one.) Gets a pink custom-made bra.

She had thought of that way before… Nurse was sentimental and yet acknowledged her colonel with nostalgia, perhaps a touch of Melancholia (a technical term.) Checked out a Tarzan movie.

The world is dizzy: red hands, red numbers, red cars racing.

(She walks along Bedford, going north. Sees herself in a window. Takes out a brilliant lip gloss. What else would you have done if you were in her place?)

(Sees young women, with long black skirts. My mind is a parenthesis going Nowhere.)

Her friends whispered:

"Mother died of a cancer of memory."

And then The Rains Came.

Umbrellas popped up.

My second language.

The Captain thought better, and ordered us to hide under his desk.

THE COLONEL's DREAM INTERRUPTED

....
.... Trauma
....
....

....
....

"I want you to recite passage number 43 from one of Apollinaire's porno novels."

Someone else might have been doing the very Same Thing.

Voices choked on the return of a memo. How connected we are!

(Here, I would like to insert an appropriate quote something like… but

I've forgotten which one!

Where were the dried-out petals of a forgotten "past"? Sometimes, I dreamt of a Baude-laire's perfume, remembered in a

commode (was that true?)

When one of our prisoners died on the table, we shut off the water and, all of us, all of us, went out for a smoke.

I heard myself saying something about Trotsky's literary essays…but which one?

BIG BEN (once more

it's muted language.)

THE INTERVIEWER

....

....

Paul Ricoeur smiles: "L'analogie de l'égo."

I live in perpetual negation, an expectation? A memory of memory?

....

I might add...But I've forgotten what I was about to add!! Please forgive me. I'm having holes remembering even the Immediate! Call it a

trauma. Insist on resolving what seems to be a nothing. Water emptied in the shower. After washing her hair, strands in the tub.

"O for the touch of a vanished YOU,

And the sound of an Orchestra that is still."

The Orient Express refused to have its sides painted by Graduate students of the Ecole des Beaux Arts in Moscow.

A grad. suggested a reading in Latin of

Catullus 32...   (Translated by Carl

Cesar.)

home, warm it up,

But just stay

out nine straight fucks for me. And spread

right now, in fact?   Who will dare refute me?

....
....

Anything to dissolve the Present.

"Can't you hear those bells, bells,
bells?"

" Does memory block out itself?"

Foucault writes: "Memory is a syncopated

recapitulation of the frontal lobe."

The place was heated, as if a reading before a firing squad.

When the interrogator entered the room, there was a slight breeze
and, all of us, sitting there, shivered a bit. An affirmative voice:
"Please identify your selves for the record. You first," He pointed to
Agatha. An answer: "here's the beginning of my novel and its precipi-
tous

conclusion: I Smelled Bushels of Blood splattering on the table."

....
....

....
....

....

....

If André Breton and Jacques Vaché did it, why not do it yourself?
(To cheer us up, an unknown voice declared that John Taylor,
known

as House,

Weighed 500 pounds at 6-11.)

At least, had we a text in front of us? No such luck. You could hear
the ticking of an old -fashioned camera shutting down.

TICKTICKTICK LIKELIKELIKE

an old fashioned tune always, but ...

....

....

....

.... Here's a
memory barrier?

At least   Remember empty spaces.

                                        Silence.

In perfect alexandrines, Racine, this morning, claimed drones fired two missiles
at militants, and set fire to four of their copters, each valued at 23 million. A top
general in the Pakistani army was heard to say:

                                        "The next drone I hear, I'll

shoot it down."

I too, under other circumstances, would hover over the same, but do not

    Tell anyone, especially on Clover Street.

    John Ruskin writes: "The night was

    wild with snow…"

    What if apples were to ripen again? They're all primitive rejects.

    *(Dickens: "Stick to facts, facts, facts."). All is in the transgression of prose
and, for example, finding oneself outside the sliding doors of the mind.
HER last Words, probably borrowed*

    *from one of her novels, Circa 1930. She said, out loud, in an historical
voice, like in a realist novel, pleasing some Eastern European Leftist
critic:*

      " I'll never forget our Marxist conversations."

                                        In the meantime…

(I've always, always wondered what that "meantime"

Meant.)

....
.... (Leaps of behavior?)

....

(Mystic terrorists surrounded him.)

(HERE, Insert your own
thoughts.)

In a government elevator, which went nowhere, he thought he
heard a silence.

I've forgotten: was it blank or did it,

Sometimes, I can't, for the life of me, You
as a...

Can't find An
appropriate

Memory, forgot-
ten

192

A voice
invents
an

Invisible dream

A description of a "what"

Dreams of an officer's next invention.

NOW PLEASE

CHOOSE:

OVID: "And Love is on my side,
who gives to you myself as a gift..." (Memory?)

EZRA POUND: "And then down to
the ship..." (If you agree.)

ELVIS: "Memo-
ries..." (That's all, folks!)

(not quite)

(A wave of a magic wand.)

LET's silence memory, AT LEAST for now.)

          Say, why not consider memory a deceptive consolation, a self-imposed
deception,

      An artful turn, a so-called void to reign over a void

    undisputed? Then, an invention of a past failed, or a double
spaced fiction?

                  Would that satisfy an otherwise
hollowness?

A touch invented, as far as the eye could wander? Disavow
the previous. But think of it as a naked valve or an invisible
mirror, nailed to the mind. An envelope not yet opened.

What else could it have been?

Try this one for size:

Memory is a broken necklace, a single pearl's echo, as if it
concealed the totality of the whole?

194

Or

Memory as a realm, or an image-making realm.

Or might it be (while we're at it) a testimony of self-immolation, a virtuous feel for abstraction? A clawed one?

TRIPLE SPACE

(Vox clamantis in Dersto)

(Stephen King once said the perfect monster was the one you make in your mind.)

THE END

32589129R00126

Made in the USA
Charleston, SC
22 August 2014